First World War
and Army of Occupation
War Diary
France, Belgium and Germany

59 DIVISION
176 Infantry Brigade
Royal Sussex Regiment
17th Battalion
1 May 1918 - 30 April 1919

WO95/3021/11

The Naval & Military Press Ltd
www.nmarchive.com
Published in association with The National Archives

Published by

The Naval & Military Press Ltd

Unit 10 Ridgewood Industrial Park,

Uckfield, East Sussex,

TN22 5QE England

Tel: +44 (0) 1825 749494

www.naval-military-press.com

www.nmarchive.com

This diary has been reprinted in facsimile from the original. Any imperfections are inevitably reproduced and the quality may fall short of modern type and cartographic standards.

© **Crown Copyright**
Images reproduced by permission of The National Archives, London, England, 2015.

Contents

Document type	Place/Title	Date From	Date To
Heading	WO95/3021/11		
Heading	176th Brigade 59th Division France 17th Battalion Royal Sussex Regt 1918 May-1919 Apl Formed in France		
Heading	17th Bn. 176 Bn 59th Div May 1918 Dec		
Heading	War Diary of 5th Prov G.G. Battn. 17th G. Battn. Royal Sussex Regt From May 1st 1918 To May 31st 1918 Vol 1		
War Diary	Fosseux P.10.d.	01/05/1918	18/05/1918
War Diary	Fosseux P.10.d. Lattre St. Quentin J 23 d.	19/05/1918	19/05/1918
War Diary	Lattre St. Quentin 51.c. J 23. d. Magnicourt En-Comte 36 B O34	20/05/1918	20/05/1918
War Diary	Magnicourt En-Comte 36 B O34 Bailleul Les Pernes 36 B. B 21	21/05/1918	21/05/1918
War Diary	Bailleul Les Pernes 36 B. B 21	22/05/1918	23/05/1918
War Diary	Bailleul Les Pernes 36 B. B 21 Therouanne 36 D L 28b	24/05/1918	24/05/1918
War Diary	Therouanne 36 D L 28b Clarques 36 A G 13 D1.1	25/05/1918	25/05/1918
War Diary	Clarques 36A G 13d1.1	26/05/1918	31/05/1918
Heading	War Diary of 17th G. Bn. Royal Sussex Regt From 1st June 1918 To 30th June 1918 Vol 2		
War Diary	Clarques 36A G 13d1.1	01/06/1918	16/06/1918
War Diary	Beaumetz Lez Aire 36 D X 26	16/06/1918	30/06/1918
Heading	War Diary of 17th Bn. Royal Sussex Regt. From July 1st 1918 To July 31st 1918 Vol 3		
War Diary	Beaumetz Les Aire	01/07/1918	08/07/1918
War Diary	Sains Les Pernes	09/07/1918	23/07/1918
War Diary	Bellacourt	23/07/1918	31/07/1918
Heading	War Diary of 17th Bn. Royal Sussex Regiment From-August 1st 1918 To August 31st 1918 Vol 4		
War Diary	Mercatel	01/08/1918	02/08/1918
War Diary	Gouy En Artois	03/08/1918	07/08/1918
War Diary	Bretencourt	08/08/1918	14/08/1918
War Diary	Chat Maigre	15/08/1918	20/08/1918
War Diary	Mercatel	21/08/1918	23/08/1918
War Diary	Beaumetz	24/08/1918	24/08/1918
War Diary	Lillers	25/08/1918	25/08/1918
War Diary	St. Hilars	26/08/1918	26/08/1918
War Diary	Busnes	27/08/1918	31/08/1918
Heading	War Diary of 17th The Royal Sussex Regiment From 1st Sept. 1918 To 30th Sept. 1918		
War Diary	Robecq	01/09/1918	02/09/1918
War Diary	River Lawe	03/09/1918	07/09/1918
War Diary	Pont Duhem	08/09/1918	09/09/1918
War Diary	11f Line	10/09/1918	13/09/1918
War Diary	Le Drumez Sector	14/09/1918	28/09/1918
War Diary	Picantin Sector	29/09/1918	30/09/1918
Heading	War Diary of 17th Bn. Royal Sussex Regiment From 1st Oct. 1918 To 31st Octr. 1918 Vol 6		
War Diary	Picantin Sector	01/10/1918	05/10/1918
War Diary	Wez Macquart	06/10/1918	10/10/1918

War Diary	Erquinghem Sector	11/10/1918	15/10/1918
War Diary	Wez Macquart	16/10/1918	16/10/1918
War Diary	Lommelet	17/10/1918	17/10/1918
War Diary	Le Marcq River	18/10/1918	18/10/1918
War Diary	Forzeau	19/10/1918	19/10/1918
War Diary	Chauny	20/10/1918	21/10/1918
War Diary	Toufflers	22/10/1918	31/10/1918
Heading	War Diary of 17th Bn. Royal Sussex Regiment From 1st Nov. 1918 To 30th Nov. 1918 Vol 7		
War Diary	Toufflers	01/11/1918	09/11/1918
War Diary	Quatre Vents	10/11/1918	10/11/1918
War Diary	Vellaines	11/11/1918	12/11/1918
War Diary	Quatre Vents	13/11/1918	15/11/1918
War Diary	Willems	16/11/1918	16/11/1918
War Diary	Thumesnil	17/11/1918	30/11/1918
Heading	War Diary of 17th Bn. The Royal Sussex Regiment From Dec. 1st 1918 To Dec. 31st 1918 Vol 8		
War Diary	Lille	01/12/1918	06/12/1918
War Diary	Maisnil Les Ruitz	06/12/1918	31/12/1918
Miscellaneous	Administrative Instructions 4th Dec 1918	04/12/1918	04/12/1918
Operation(al) Order(s)	17 Battalion Royal Sussex Regt. Order No. C 19	05/12/1918	05/12/1918
Miscellaneous	17th Royal Sussex Regt Move Order By L. Coln N. Collard No C. 30	20/12/1918	20/12/1918
Heading	War Diary of 17th Bn. The Royal Sussex Regiment From January 1st-January 31st 1919 Vol 9		
War Diary	Maisnil Les Ruitz	01/01/1919	05/01/1919
War Diary	Staple	06/01/1919	30/01/1919
War Diary	Dunkirk	31/01/1919	31/01/1919
Heading	War Diary February 1919 17th Batt. Royal Sussex Regt. Vol 10		
War Diary	Mardyck Camp Dunkirk	01/02/1919	28/02/1919
Heading	War Diary of 17th Royal Sussex Regt. From March 1st 1919 To March 31st 1919 Vol 11		
War Diary	Mardyck Dunkerque	01/03/1919	11/03/1919
War Diary	Pont de Petit Synthe	12/03/1919	24/03/1919
War Diary	Mardyck Dunkerque	25/03/1919	31/03/1919
Heading	War Diary of 17th Bn Royal Sussex Regt From 1st April 1919 To 30 April 1919 Vol 12		
War Diary	Mardyck	01/04/1919	30/04/1919

w as/3021/M

176TH BRIGADE
59TH DIVISION

FRANCE

1.7TH BATTALION

ROYAL SUSSEX REGT.

MAY — DEC 1918

1918 MAY — 1919 DEC

FORMED IN FRANCE

FROM - EGYPT
TO A 75 DIVISION — 234 BDE

France

17th Bn. 176 Bde 59° Div
{ May 1918
{ Dec.

Army Form C. 2118.

17/59

WAR DIARY
or
INTELLIGENCE SUMMARY

(Erase heading not required.)

Vol I

Original

Confidential

War Diary
of
5th Army L.G. Battn. — 17th G. Battn. Royal Irish Rifles

From May 1st 1918
to May 31st 1918

Miss West

7.1

WAR DIARY

5TH PROV. GARRISON GUARDS. BN. → 17TH G.B. ROYAL SUSSEX. REGT.

Place	Date	Hour	
FOSSEUX P.10.d.	1918 May 1st		Ref. Map. France. Sheet 51.c. Scale 1:40,000. The Battalion in camp and employed in deepening the G.H.Q. line. On this day work on parapets was discontinued, and every attention given to deepening trenches, revetting fire steps, working on forward posts, and completing communication trenches. Strength of Battalion 14 Officers & 928 Other Ranks. Weather Fine.
do.	2nd		Weather Fine. Digging continued, and party detailed to dig a cable trench from FOSSEUX 51.c. P.10.a to AVESNES LE COMTE. 51.c. J.21.
do.	3rd		Weather Fine. Digging continued. Every available man was put to work on the trenches.
do.	4th		Weather Fine. Work concentrated on deepening fire bays and revetting fire steps. Capt. W. Kelly-Patterson. R.A.Ch.D. reported for duty as M.O.
do.	5th		Weather Fine. Church Parades for Presbyterians & Roman Catholics. 6/0 works Parade. 13 Officers reported for duty. Major H. Armitage. K.O.r.y.L.I. att. Ef. Trench Labour Corps. Lieuts. G. Lilly, while. Edmony Regt. & 2nd Lieuts. H.J. Brennan, H.J. Beckett, J.L. Cartwright, J.R. Finnegan, A.G. Brown, R.E. Bennison, R. Darling, J.M. Edmonds, G.H. Fleming, & G. Cahill, all Labour Corps.
do.	6th		Weather Fine. Digging continued, and party detailed to assist Australian Tunnelling Company at P.9. d.8.9. Two platoons received instruction in musketry.

Place	Date	Hour	
FOSSEUX P.10.d.	May 7th		Weather Wet. Digging & training continued. Inspection of Small Box Respirators by the Brigade Gas Officer. Lt. T.J.Ch. Tebbutt 1st/Reg. Yar. Bat. Suffolk Rgt. reported for duty.
do	8th		Weather Fine. Digging & training continued at 11.0 a.m. Inspection by the Army Commander at 2.15 p.m.
do	9th		Weather Fine. Digging & training continued. 21 Other ranks reported as reinforcements from No. 3 E.B. Depot.
do	10th		Weather Fine. Digging & training continued. Bayonet Fighting Competition at 11.0 a.m. Guard Mounting Competition at 12.0 noon. Lieut. & Qr.Mr. Booth was admitted to Hospital & struck off the strength. 2nd Lt. A.J. Brown and M. Carlisle were attached to No.1 Pro: Garrison Guard Battalion
do	11th		Weather Fine. 40 Other ranks reported as reinforcements from No. 3 E.B. Depot. 16 Other Ranks reported as reinforcements from 912. A.E. (A.G.) Company.
do	12th		Weather Fine. Church Parade at 10.45 a.m. No work or training.
do	13th		Weather Wet. Digging & training continued.
do	14th		Weather Fine. do.
do	15th		Weather Fine. Digging & training continued. The 176th Infantry Brigade took over command from the 197th Infantry Brigade at 3.0 p.m. On 15.5.1918. Capt. E.H.Black R.A.Ch.D. & Lt. B.Robinson 1/9 Manchester Rgt. were withdrawn to report to VII Corps School.
do	16th		Weather Fine. Digging & training continued.
do	17th		Weather Fine. Digging & training continued. 2nd Lt. L.A.Hunt. Labour Corps reported for duty.

Place	Date	Hour		
FOSSEUX P10 d.	1918 May 18th		Weather fine. Digging & training continued. 2nd Lieut. J.W. Wake Suffolk Regt. evacuated "sick" and struck off the strength.	A/B
FOSSEUX P10 d.	19th		Weather fine. Church Parade 9.30 a.m. No digging or training. 2/Lt. E.L. Platt 2/6 Manchester Regt reported for duty as Batt. Transport Officer. Capt. (Rev.) E.A.C. Rattray A.P.10. reported for duty as Padre. The Battalion left FOSSEUX at 5.30 p.m. and marched to ZATTRE-ST-QUENTIN where it was billeted for the night.	A/B
ZATTRE-ST QUENTIN. C.723.d. MAGNICOURT-EN-COMTE. 36 B O.34.	20th		Weather fine. The Battalion left York Roads J22.c.95.00. at 4.0 a.m. and marched via NOYELLE VION, IZEL-LEZ-HAMEAU, Sioux Roads D4.a 15.90. TINQUES, CHELERS to MAGNICOURT-EN-COMTE. Sheet 36B 1:40,000 O.34. where it was billeted for the night.	A/B
MAGNICOURT EN-COMTE 36.B O.34. BAILLEUL-LES-PERNES. C.B. B.21.	21st		Weather fine. the Battalion left York Roads O.29.b.0.9. at 5.30 a.m. and marched via HOUNEZIN, LA COMTE, OURTON, CAMBEZAIN CHATEZAIN, PERNES, to BAILLEUL-LES-PERNES where it was billeted for the night.	A/B
BAILLEUL LES PERNES 36 B B.21.	22nd		Weather fine. Battalion resting. Inspection given in Musketry & Arms Drill.	A/B
	23rd		Weather fine. Same as 22nd	A/B

Place	Date	Hour		
BAILLEUL-LES-PERNES. 36.B.B.21.	1918 May 24		Weather Wet. The battalion left BAILLEUL-LES-PERNES. 36.B.B.21. at 5.0 a.m. and marched via NEDONCHELLE, AUCHY-AU-BOIS, ESTREE BLANCHE to THEROUANNE where it was billeted for the night. Four officers (2nd Lts. J.H. Loot, R.A. Frame, J.G. Sinclair, & H.G.A. Haydon all Labour Corps) reported for duty.		4/11/3
THEROUANNE. 36.D. I.28.b.	25th		Weather fine. The battalion left THEROUANNE at 10 a.m. and marched to CLARQUES. where it went into camp. at Sheet 36 : 1:40.000 G.13.d.1.1. The day was spent in pitching camp. 2nd Lieut J.H. Cahill was appointed Transport Officer to the Battalion. Lieut L.L. Platt 2/6 Manchester Regt. was withdrawn to report to 199 Infantry Brigade.		4/11/3
CLARQUES. 36.A G.13.d.1.1.	26th		Weather fine. Church Parade at 10.30 a.m. Parapets built round tents for protection against aircraft bombs. 2nd Lieut G.J. Davies conducted draft of 40 other ranks incapable of using fire arms to 62nd Labour Company. Lieut & Qmr. J.W. Rowley 1st/6th Staffs. Regt. reported for duty & is attached to the Battalion. The designation of the battalion changed to 17th GARRISON BATTALION. ROYAL SUSSEX REGIMENT.		14/11/3
do.	27th		The battalion commenced digging the H.B. Line, REBECQ, sub-sector under No. 469 Coy. R.E. Weather fine.		4/11/3

Place	Date	Hour		
LARQUES. 36 A G 13 d.i.i	May 28th		Weather fine. Digging continued. One hours training in Platoon, Company & Close Order Drill, Musketry, rapid loading, fire orders, fire direction & control and Arms Drill. 2nd Lieut J. McMahin 1st(Res) Garrison Batt. Suffolk Regt reported for duty. 2nd Lieut D. Carlisle returned from 11th Garr. Batt. Worcestershire Regt.	AAB
do.	29th		Weather fine. Digging & training continued	AAB
do.	30th		Weather fine. Same as 29th	AAB
do.	31st		Weather fine. Same as 29th. Inspection by Divisional Commander. Strength of Battalion. 33 Officers, 923 Other Ranks.	AAB

W R Empey
Lieut. Colonel.
Commanding 17th Garrison Battalion
Royal Sussex Regiment.

Army Form C. 2118.

WAR DIARY
or
INTELLIGENCE SUMMARY
(Erase heading not required.)

Vol 2

Confidential

Original

War Diary
of
1st G. Bn Royal Sussex Regt

From 1st June 1915.
to 30th June 1915.

WAR DIARY

17TH GARRISON BN ROYAL SUSSEX REGT:

PLACE	DATE	HOUR	
LARQUES. 6A 13 d I.I.	1918 June		REF. MAP. FRANCE SHEET 36A. 1:40.000. SUMMARY. From the 1st to 14th June the Battalion was digging the "BB" Line. REBECQ Sub-sector at CLARQUES. and was also doing one hours training a day in Platoon, Company & Close Order Drill, Fire Orders, Fire Direction & Control, Musketry, Rapid Loading & Arms Drill. The Battalion rested on the 15th June & marched to BEAUMETZ-LEZ-AIRE on the 16th June. From the 17th to 30th June it was training at BEAUMETZ-LEZ-AIRE. The re-organisation & training of the Battalion was considerably handicapped by 1. The presence of 138 Other Ranks of Categories BII & BIII who left the Battalion on 25th June. 2 An outbreak of P.U.O. which first appeared about the middle of June & was greatly increased by the hot B I reinforcements who arrived on the 25th June & necessitated 136 men being isolated from the 25th to 30th June. 3. The large number N.C.O's sent on course of instruction. HWB
do.	1st		Weather fine. Battalion digging BB Line Rebecq Sub-sector under C/s 469. Coy. R.E. One hours training. Strength of Battalion 33. Officers. 724 Other Ranks. HWB
do.	2nd		Weather fine. Digging continued. No training. No Church Parade. Inspection of Camp by A.D.M.S. 1 Officer left the Battalion. 1 Officer reported for duty. HWB

PLACE	DATE	HOUR		
CLARQUES	1918			
36 A	JUNE			
c.13 d.11	3rd		Weather fine. Digging & training continued.	H/B
do	4th		Weather fine. Digging & training continued.	H/B
do	5th		Weather fine. do.	H/B
do	6th		Weather fine. do.	H/B
do	7th		Weather fine. do.	H/B
do	8th		Weather fine. do.	H/B
do	9th		Weather fine. No Church Parade. Trenches manned in battle order.	H/B
do	10th		Weather fine. Digging & training continued.	H/B
do	11th		Weather fine. Digging & training continued. Inspection by	H/B
do	12th		Inspector of Drafts. Weather fine. Digging & training continued. Inspection by Inspector of Drafts. Lecture to Officers on "Trench Routine" by Brig: Gen: J. G. Rolfe M.S.O. Cmdg. 176th Infantry Brigade.	H/B
do	13th		Weather fine. "B" Coy digging. "A" "C" & "D" Companies training. Inspection at 5.30 p.m. by Lt. Gen. Sir. W. E. Peyton. K.C.B; K.C.V.O; D.S.O; Cmdg. 10th Corps; accompanied by Brig: Gen: L.H.L James C.B; C.M.G; Cmdg. 59th Division & Brig. Gen. J.G. Rolfe D.S.O. Cmdg. 176th Infantry Brigade.	H/B
do	14th		Weather fine. "A" & "B" Companies digging. "C" & "D" Boys training.	H/B
do	15th		Weather fine. No digging or training.	C/H/B
do	16th		Weather fine.	H/B
		3.55 a.m.	Movement Orders received from 176th Infantry Brigade.	
		4.5 a.m.	Battalion Movement Order issued to O.C. Companies	
		5.30 a.m.	Battalion left CLARQUES. Took Roads F.29.c.3.8. & marched via	
BEAUMETZ			THEROUANNE & BOMY to BEAUMETZ-LEZ-AIRE.	
LEZ-AIRE			BEAUMETZ-LEZ-AIRE. Arrived at 10.15 a.m.	H/B
36 D X 26				

EAUMETZ-LES-AIRE 6D X 26	1918 JUNE		
	17th	Weather Fine. Commenced training in Drill, Musketry, Physical Training, Bayonet fighting, Gas Drill, Firing & Tactical Exercises. Lectures given by Commanding Officer, Company & Platoon Commanders.	
	18th	Weather Fine. Training continued. C.O. attended conference at Divisional Hqrs.	
	19th	Weather Showery. Training continued. One Officer reported for duty.	
	20th	Weather Showery. Training continued. Inspection by Maj. Gen. Sir R.D. Whigham, K.C.B, D.S.O, Comdg 59th Division.	
	21st	Weather Fine. Route March 6 miles in morning. Training 2.0 to 4.0 p.m. Inspection of Billets by A.Q.M.G. 59th Division.	
	22nd	Weather Fine. The whole Battalion fired on the Rifle Range. One Officer attached to the Battalion as an instructor.	
	23rd	Weather Fine. No Church Parade. Battalion fired on the Rifle Range.	
	24th	Weather Showery. Training continued.	
	25th	Weather Fine. Route March 7 miles in morning. Training 2.0 to 4.0 p.m. One Officer & 138 Other Ranks B.I. & B.III. left for Base. 144 Other Ranks joined for duty from O/c Reinforcements. 136 O.R. revaluated on account of P.U.O.	
	26th	Weather Fine. Training continued. Capt. R.W.H. Venour took over command during the absence on leave of Lt. Col. W.R. Campion D.S.O. 47 O.R. in Hospital.	
	27th	Weather Fine. Battalion practiced relief of trenches.	
	28th	Weather Fine. Training continued. Maj. Gen. Sir R.D. Whigham, K.C.B, D.S.O, Inspected the Battalion in training.	
	29th	Weather Fine. Same as 28th. 3 Officers joined & 1 Officer left the Battalion.	
	30th	Weather Fine. Church Parade. Lt. Col. W.R. Campion D.S.O, resumed command. Strength. 34 Officers. 913 Other Ranks.	

W.R. Campion
Lieut. Colonel.
Comdg 17th Gan. Bn. Royal Sussex Regiment.

WAR DIARY
~~INTELLIGENCE SUMMARY~~
(Erase heading not required.)

Army Form C. 2118.

CONFIDENTIAL.

WAR DIARY
OF
14th Bn. ROYAL SUSSEX REGT.

From:- JULY 1st 1918.
To:- JULY 31st 1918.

WAR DIARY

17th Battn ROYAL SUSSEX REGT

PLACE	DATE	HOUR	SUMMARY OF EVENTS + INFORMATION	REMARKS &c
BEAUMETZ-LES-AIRE	1918. JULY. 1st		REF. MAP. Weather fine. 8 mile Route March in the morning. Training afternoon. Tactical scheme for officers & men in the afternoon. Strength of Battalion. 34 Officers + 316 O.R.S.	
do	" 2		Weather fine. P.T. & B.T. Peloton + Coy Training in Musketry, Gas Drill, & x Drill Bridge. 2/Lt. Sinclair admitted to Hospital. Capt. Wenham a/adjt - vice Capt. Page on leave. Training as 2nd July. 59th Brigade Transferred to Cav. Corps 1st ARMY from X Corps.	
do	" 3			
do	" 4		Weather fine. Battalion Parade & Training as 2nd July.	
do	" 5		Weather fine. Massing of Trenches (per operation orders)	
do	" 6		Weather fine. Morning Training. Afternoon Range firing (1.30 p.m to 6 p.m) 500 yds 1st Class figure, 5 Rounds, Lying, an open Bayonet figure 5 Rounds, Bayonet Unfixed	
do	" 7		Weather fine. Church Parade. No Training	
do	" 8		Move Battalion Orders No 1 received 9/4/5. Bde Order No 113 Notes 8th July. 1918. 2/Lt Sinclair returned to duty. 17th Inf Bde order No 112	
SAINS-LES-PERNES	" 9		Weather fine. Battalion marched to SAINS-LES-PERNES. for operation order No 1 arrived at 9.20 a.m. Location of Billets A + B Coys at SAINS-LES-PERNES. H. Qrs, C + D Coy + Transport moved to PRESSY-LE-PERNES arrived at 12.0 P.M.	
do	" 10		Weather showery. Training under Battn arrangements. (per programme) do	
do	" 11		Weather fine. do	

WAR DIARY.

11th. BATTN. ROYAL SUSSEX REGT.

PLACE.	DATE	HOUR	SUMMARY OF EVENTS + INFORMATION.	REMARKS &c.
SAINS-LES-PERNES.	July 12.		Weather wet. Training under Battn. arrangements (per Programme) Lecture to officers on "Holding the Line" by Brig Genl. T.G. Cope D.S.O. Commanding 116. Inf. Bde.	
do	" 13		Weather fine. Training as per Programme. Battalion inspected in the morning by Gen Sir H.S. Horne K.C.B. K.C.M.G. Commanding 1st. Army.	
do	" 14		Weather Showery. Church Parades.	
do	" 15		Weather fine. Route march per Programme. A + B Coys moved to PRESSY-LE-PERNES.	
do	" 16		Capt. Wenham returned to 39th Division.	
do	" 17		Weather fine, & Very Hot. Training 8 to 10. Demonstration by Peabour (10/1/12 & 2/10 H.)	
do	" 18		Weather fine. Training as per Programme. Capt Venour to Base for Medl. Board.	
do	" 19		do (7.0 A.M to 10 P.M.)	
do	" 20		do	
do	" 21		"Stand to" Manning Trenches 7 to 12 P.M. Weather fine. A + D Coys. Training. B + C Coys. Embussed for Kruchell at 1-0. P.M. for a 2 day tour in the line at LA BASSÉE Salient with SW B's "C" Coy into the Trenches quite successful, no casualties. "B" were with 1st Gloster, 12st. Division.	
do	" 22		Weather fine. Church Parades. No Training. B + C Coys in the line.	
do	" 23		Weather fine. 2 Coys in line returned to PRESSY-LES-PERNES.	
BELLACOURT.	" 24		Weather Very Wet. Battalion embussed & came to BELLACOURT. Pouring rain all day. Fine return debussing.	
do			Weather Good. Senior Officers reconnoitred line. Brig Gen spoke to the Battn at 5 P.M.	

WAR DIARY.

17th BATTN ROYAL SUSSEX REGT.

PLACE.	DATE.	HOUR.	SUMMARY OF EVENTS + INFORMATION	REMARKS &c
BELLACOURT	July 25		Weather fine. Battn relieved 2nd Q. Victorian R Can. Regt in R. Support area.	
"	" 26		Weather fair. Battn still in close support.	
"	" 27		Weather wet-rain. Battn still in R. Support. working parties found from all Coys.	
"	" 28		Weather morning wet, evening fine. Evening Battn proceeded from close support to front area. Relief Good, but slow 3 Casualties Kissed	
"	" 29		Weather fine. Local Showers. Battn still in front Sector. Br. Gen A Holdane visited Battalion in line. C.S.M Pink "D"Coy died of wounds received (previous night). Battn sent out Three Patrols, no result.	
"	" 30		Weather fine Battalion still in front-line.	do
"	" 31			do

W R Lamp[?] Lieut-Colonel
Commanding 17th Battn
Royal Sussex Regt

Army Form C. 2118.

WAR DIARY
INTELLIGENCE SUMMARY.
(Erase heading not required.)

176/59

106 4

J.4

CONFIDENTIAL.

WAR DIARY
of
11th Bn. ROYAL SUSSEX REGIMENT

From – August 1st 1918
To – August 31st 1918

ORIGINAL

WAR DIARY
14th Batt. ROYAL SUSSEX REGT.
INTELLIGENCE SUMMARY. AUGUST 1918.

Army Form C. 2118.

(Erase heading not required.)

Place	Date	Hour	Summary of Events and Information	Remarks and references to Appendices
MERCATEL	1		Weather FINE. Batt in FRONT LINE.	REF. MAP. 1:20.000 SHEET 51BSW
"			2/Lt. J.G. SINCLAIR + 4 O.R's accidentally wounded on patrol.	
"	2		Weather VERY WET. Trenches extremely muddy + difficult.	176 Bde odu.No.120
"			NIGHT 2/3 176 Bde relieved in line by 14th Bde. 14th SUSSEX by 36th NORTHUMBERLAND FUSILIERS.	dated 31/7/18
OUY-EN-ARTOIS	3		Weather FINE. Batt. entrained at BLAIRVILLE on being relieved from FRONT LINE. Detrained at BAVINCOURT + marched to GOUY-EN-ARTOIS to billets.	REF. MAP. LENS. ED. 2. 1:100.000
		2.P.M.	Whole battalion reported present in billets.	
			2/Lts. R. GREENWOOD + 2/Lt. S. BRAYBROOKS reported for duty.	
"	4		Weather FINE. No Parades. Batt rest clean up after trenches	
"	5		Weather FINE. Cleaning up + re-organization	
		9.35 P.M.	Practice FIRE-ALARM.	
			2/Lts. C. REDMAN. W.T. WRIGHT, F.S. CHERRY, F. TURNER, C.R.M. FRY, F. CROSS, J.R. BUCKLAND, report for duty.	
"	6		Weather FINE. Practice alarm. "ASSEMBLE + FALL IN". TIME ½ HOUR	

WAR DIARY
or
INTELLIGENCE SUMMARY.
(Erase heading not required.)

17th ROYAL SUSSEX REGT.

AUGUST 1918

Army Form C. 2118.

Place	Date	Hour	Summary of Events and Information	Remarks and references to Appendices
OUYEN-ARTOIS	6 (CONT)		after order to "FALL IN". Specialist & Coy TRAINING. LECTURE to officers "TRENCH ROUTINE" by Bde C.O.	
"	7		Weather FINE. Am. resting. LECTURE to officers by G.O.C. DIV. 2/Lt Y.A. SARGENT, S.O. GRANT, S.E. GOSHAWK report for duty	
BRETENCOURT	8	9.40AM	Weather FINE. Inspection of Batt by G.O.C VI CORPS. 1/6th Bde relieved 17th Bde in line night 8/9. 17th SUSSEX in Bde	1/6 Bde Order No.12 d/d 7/8/13
"		5.30PM	RESERVE at BRETENCOURT. Batt reported all present in billets at BRETENCOURT.	
"	9	7.30PM	Weather FINE. Batt in Bde RESERVE. Ordinary training continued. Practice "STAND TO".	
"	10		Lts. R. BULLOCK, S.J. WILLARD & 2/Lt F.H. JENNER report for duty. Weather FINE. Batt in Bde RESERVE. Specialist & company training. COMMAND. Lt. Col. W.R. CAMPION D.S.O. proceeded to take over command of 11th ROYAL SUSSEX REGT. Col. W.F. BARKER C.M.G. D.S.O. WORCESTER REGT assumed command of Batt.	
"	11		Weather FINE. Batt in Bde RESERVE. CHURCH PARADE. NAIL-SALVAGE MOVEMENT	

WAR DIARY or INTELLIGENCE SUMMARY

17th Batt. Royal Sussex Regt.
August 1918

Army Form C. 2118.

Place	Date	Hour	Summary of Events and Information	Remarks and references to Appendices
RETENCOURT	12		Weather FINE. Bn in Bde RESERVE. Coy & Specialists training. BfW	
	13		Weather FINE. Bn in Bde RESERVE. Coy & Specialists training. BfW	
	14	8.30 P.M.	Weather FINE. Bn moved up to CHAT MAISRE in Bde SUPPORT LINE & relieved 25th KINGS LIVERPOOL REGT.	
		10.30 P.M.	Relief reported complete. BfW	
CHAT MAISRE	15		Weather FINE. Batt at CHAT MAISRE SUPPORT LINE. BfW	REF. MAP. 1:20,000 SHEET 51B. S.W.
	16		Weather FINE. Batt still at CHAT MAISRE SUPPORT LINE. BfW	
	17		Weather SHOWERY. Batt still at CHAT MAISRE SUPPORT LINE. BfW	
	18		Weather FINE. Batt still at CHAT MAISRE SUPPORT LINE. CAPT. R.H. HUTTON reported for duty with Batt. BfW	
	19		Weather FINE. Batt still at CHAT MAISRE SUPPORT LINE. BfW	
	20	6 P.M.	Weather FINE. Batt moved up into FRONT LINE, LEFT SECTOR and relieved 25th Batt. KINGS LIVERPOOL REGT. Relief fairly good.	
		11 P.M.	Relief reported complete. BfW	
MERCATEL	21		Weather FINE. Batt still in FRONT LINE, LEFT SECTOR. BfW	
	22		Weather HOT. Batt still in FRONT LINE. BfW. W.E. WEEKS reported for duty. BfW	

WAR DIARY or INTELLIGENCE SUMMARY

11th Batt. ROYAL SUSSEX REGT.
AUGUST 1918

Army Form C. 2118.

Place	Date	Hour	Summary of Events and Information	Remarks and references to Appendices
ERCATEL	23	10 p.m.	Weather FINE. Batt left FRONT LINE not relieved by anyone & marched by companies to BEAUMETZ. Bivouaced for night in field by ARRAS-BOULON'S ROAD.	
			night 22/23. Batt. suffered numerous casualties through enemies shell gas. Sgts. E. TURNER, S.A. SARGENT, T.R. FINNIGAN, B. O'REILLY NUGENT, & 6 l.O.R's sent to Hospital as reported gas casualties. Sgd. whilst in line, a good amount of salvage was collected. Sgd.	
BEAUMETZ	24	11 a.m.	Weather SHOWERY. Batt reported present in BIVOUAC AREA.	
		9.30 a.m.	Batt marched to HABRET.	
		12 noon	Batt arrived HABRET.	
		4 p.m.	Batt entrained at HABRET STATION. Sgd.	R.E.P. MAP 1:40,000 SHEET 36A. EDT. 6.
HILLERS	25	3 p.m.	Weather HOT. Batt arrived at HILLERS STATION & marched to ST. HILARIE. Sgd.	
		6 p.m.	Batt reported all present in billets at ST. HILARIE.	
ST. HILARIE	26	3.10 p.m.	Weather SHOWERY. Batt left for BUSNES, via HILLERS.	
		7 p.m.	Batt reported all present in billets at BUSNES. Sgd.	

1st Batt. ROYAL SUSSEX REGT.
1/4 Batt ROYAL SUSSEX REGT
AUGUST 1918   Army Form C. 2118.

WAR DIARY
INTELLIGENCE SUMMARY.
(Erase heading not required.)

Place	Date	Hour	Summary of Events and Information	Remarks and references to Appendices
BUSNES	27		Weather SHOWERY. Batt rested & cleaned up after trenches. 8gw	
"	28		Weather SHOWERY. Batt marched by companies to BATHS at GUARBECQUE 8gw	
"	29		Weather FINE. Specialists & Company training. Letter received from MAJOR-GEN. R.W. WHIGHAM on his leaving DIVISION 8gw	
"	30		Weather FINE. Specialists & Company training. 8gw	
"	31	5:58pm	Weather FINE. Specialists & company training. Batt moved to ROBECQ	
		9:30pm	Batt reported in billets. 'B' Coy in RESERVE LINE remainder of Batt. in ROBECQ. 2/Lt R. BULLOCK & 2/Lt R.D. CARLYLE EVAC. to hospital. Lt. G. EARLE to be A(CAPT) whilst comm'g Coy. 5/9/18. 7/Lt. G. BELLINGHAM to be A/CAPT. 1/9/18. Batt strength 31/8/18. 25 officers 684 O.R.s. 8gw	

sgd W.D. M^c^Intosh Lt. COLONEL
COMMANDING:-
1/4 ROYAL SUSSEX REGT.

Army Form C. 2118.

WAR DIARY
or
INTELLIGENCE SUMMARY.
(Erase heading not required.)

Vol 5

CONFIDENTIAL.

WAR DIARY
OF
11th BN. THE ROYAL SUSSEX REGIMENT.

FROM: 1st Sept. 1918.
TO: 30th Sept. 1918.

11th BATT. ROYAL SUSSEX REGIMENT

WAR DIARY or INTELLIGENCE SUMMARY
SEPTEMBER 1918

Army Form C. 2118.

Place	Date	Hour	Summary of Events and Information	Remarks and references to Appendices
ROBECQ	1		Weather FINE. Training as per programme & working parties. Strength 25 Off. 684 O.R's. SJW	REF. MAP 1:40,000 SHT. 36A FD 6
"	2		Weather FINE. Training as per programme. Working parties afternoon collecting SALVAGE. SJW	
OVER R. NAVE	3	2.30 p.m.	Weather FINE. Batt. moved up into DIVISIONAL SUPPORT to position on RIVER LAWE, VIA PARADIS, where the Batt. halted for 4 Hrs. POSITION taken from R.21.C.10.00 – R.15.6.10.30 LT. G. MAYCOCK M.C. struck off strength SJW	REF. MAP LESTREM EDGN 36B SF.2. 1:10,000
"	4	8.15 p.m.	Weather HOT. In accordance with 176 BDE order, line was advanced to a line running from R.17.2.C.50.00 NE along EASTERN BANK of stream running through R.22.A.00.50 to R.16.a.10.10. SJW	
"	5		Weather FINE. Batt still in DIV. SUPPORT. SJW Major ARMITAGE. H. struck off strength in accordance with D.R.O. 1436. o/3.5.18. SJW	
"	6		Weather FINE. River LAWE positions. Batt still in DIV SUPPORT SJW	

11th Batt Royal Sussex Regiment.

WAR DIARY
or
INTELLIGENCE SUMMARY.

Army Form C. 2118.

SEPTEMBER 1918.

Place	Date	Hour	Summary of Events and Information	Remarks and references to Appendices
RIVER LAWE	7	3 P.M.	Weather HOT. Batt moved up to position on La Boise. ESTAIRES ROAD & took up outpost positions from M.21.c. 10.00. exclusive to M.14.d.90.100. exclusive. 8fw. Draft of 30 O.R's taken on strength & posted to "B" Coy.	REF. MAP. AUBERS. 36. S.W.1. 1:10.000
CONT. DUHEM	8	10 AM	weather WET. Batt in outpost position. Communion Service. 8fw.	
"	9	8.15 P.M.	weather WET. Batt moved up into FRONT LINE & relieved 11th Royal Scots. C + A coy's in line. B & +c in support. Relief not good owing to bad weather conditions. 8fw.	
N.F. LINE	10		weather SHOWERY. Batt still in FRONT LINE. Situation quiet. 8fw.	
"	11		weather SHOWERY. C + D coy's relieved A + B coy's in FRONT LINE. 8fw.	
"	12		weather SHOWERY. Batt still in FRONT LINE. CAPT. PAGE + 2/Lt. FD MONDS wounded.	
"	13	9 P.M.	weather SHOWERY. Batt relieved in front line by 2/8 Durham L.I. Batt moved to Le DRUMEZ SECTOR. B + c in outpost line. A + c in reserve. 8fw.	
LE DRUMEL SECTOR	14		weather WET. Batt in LE DRUMEL SECTOR. 8fw.	

(cont.)

WAR DIARY or INTELLIGENCE SUMMARY.

Army Form C. 2118.

Place	Date	Hour	Summary of Events and Information	Remarks and references to Appendices
LE DRUMEZ Sector.	14 (CONTD)		CAPT. CARTLAND. J. taken on strength and posted as Adjutant	REF. MAP AUBERS 36. S.W.1 1/10,000
			2/Lt. LATHAM. W. taken on strength and posted to B Company.	
			2/Lt. CLARKE. G.L. taken on strength and posted to B Company.	
			One W.O. and 75 O.R's draft taken on strength.	Wm Ed
"	15		Weather SHOWERY Battalion still in LE DRUMEZ Sector	Wm Ed
"	16		Weather FINE " "	Wm Ed
"	17		Weather FINE " "	Wm Ed
			2/Lt. BUCKLAND J.R.B. - 2/Lt. CROSS. F - 2/Lt. FROWEN A.P. and 2/Lt. FRANE R.A. returned from course.	Wm Ed
"	18		Weather HOT morning BRIGADE Scheme - Afternoon Baths	Wm Ed
"	19		Weather FINE Gusty wind. - Training carried out by Companies as per training programme	Wm Ed
"	20		Weather SQUALLY and UNSETTLED - BRIGHT INTERVALS - Training carried out by Companies as per training programme	Wm Ed
"	21		Weather SQUALLY and UNSETTLED - BRIGHT INTERVALS. CAPT. BELL. W.S. evacuated to Base. Training carried out by Companies as per training programme	Wm Ed

WAR DIARY
or
INTELLIGENCE SUMMARY.
(Erase heading not required.)

Army Form C. 2118.

Place	Date	Hour	Summary of Events and Information	Remarks and references to Appendices
LE DRUHEZ sector	22		Weather. Showery with bright intervals. Still in LE DRUHEZ SECTOR. Divine Service held by Companies.	REF. MAP AUBERS 36 SW1 1/10,000
"	23		Weather Showery with bright intervals. Training carried out by Companies as per programme. Afternoon - Companies Wiring and improving positions. Defensive measures.	(initial)
"	24		Weather as yesterday - 2/Lt LATHAM W. killed in action. 2/Lt WRIGHT W.L. returned from course - 21 O.Rs struck off strength on proceeding to base for re-classification. Morning - Training carried on by Companies as per programme. Afternoon - Companies Wiring and improving positions - defensive measures. Miniature Rifle range constructed by Battalion N.E. of RIEZ BAILLEUL completed.	(initial)
"	25		Weather Squally with bright intervals. Morning - Training carried out by Companies as per programme. Afternoon - Companies Wiring and improving positions - defensive measures - L/G practice on new Miniature Rifle range.	(initial)

WAR DIARY
or
INTELLIGENCE SUMMARY.
(Erase heading not required.)

Army Form C. 2118.

Place	Date	Hour	Summary of Events and Information	Remarks and references to Appendices
LE DRUMEZ Sector	26.		Weather fine. MAJOR SIMPKINS A.M.C granted leave 27/9/18. To 11/10/18. Training carried out by Companies as per programme. Afternoon Companies wiring and improving positions. Defensive measures.	REF MAP AUBERS 36.S.W.1 1/10.000
"	27		Weather Fine with westerly wind. Training carried on by Companies and afternoon programme as yesterday.	
"	28		Weather Wet. Training carried on by Companies and afternoon programme as yesterday.	
PICANTIN SECTOR	29.	7.15 P.M.	Weather Wet. Battalion proceeded to front line taking over from 25th Royal Welch Fusiliers. Section from Piccadilly Trench on NORTH to a line running due EAST from point where Rifleman's Avenue meets RUE TILLELOY. C Company in front line A in immediate Support D Support B Reserve.	AUBERS MAP. S.W.I. 1/10 000 N 7a and C
"	30		Weather Wet. Battalion still in front line in last named Sector. Strength 31 Officers 746 O/Rs	

30/ September 1918

M.H. Parker Colonel
14th C. Service Regt.

Army Form C. 2118.

WAR DIARY
~~INTELLIGENCE SUMMARY.~~
(Erase heading not required.)

Instructions regarding War Diaries and Intelligence Summaries are contained in F. S. Regs., Part II. and the Staff Manual respectively. Title pages will be prepared in manuscript.

Place	Date	Hour	Summary of Events and Information	Remarks and references to Appendices

Vol 6

Confidential

Original

War Diary
of
11th Bn. Royal Sussex Regiment

From 1st Octr. 1918
To 31st Octr. 1918

17th Bn Royal Sussex Regt

WAR DIARY
INTELLIGENCE SUMMARY

October 1918

Army Form C. 2118.

Place	Date	Hour	Summary of Events and Information	Remarks and references to Appendices
PICANTIN SECTOR	1		Weather Fine. Battalion in front line in PICANTIN SECTOR. A patrol having reported SUTHERLAND AVENUE unoccupied by the enemy a Lewis Gun post was pushed forward. Battn strength Officers 36 Other Ranks 737 RS.	AUBERS MAP S.W.1
	2		Weather Fine. In conjunction with the 25th Bn Kings Liverpool Regt on the left and a latter of the 17th Bde on our right, the town attacked the enemy positions. The line was advanced to a depth of 3500" where they were held up owing to the battalion on right and left being unable to go any more forward RS.	N/ATn
	3	0010	Battn relieved in the line by the 20th London Regt and then returned to Faugemont Post. Battn provided to LAVENTIE and entrained for SAILLY-SUR-LA-LYS. Weather fine. Lt Holt M.C. detailed to take over duties of billet officer YACA RS.	OO.132
	4		Weather Well & windy. Battn proceeded to Thennies & relieving the 36 Bn Northumberland Fusiliers in support D Coy	OO.133

17th Bn Royal Sussex Regt

Army Form C. 2118.

WAR DIARY
or
INTELLIGENCE SUMMARY.
(Erase heading not required.)

October 1918

Place	Date	Hour	Summary of Events and Information	Remarks and references to Appendices
BRANTIN SECTOR	4		Being in close support to the front line Rgt	MAP
	5		Weather dull cloudy. Orders issued for Bn to pass through 26th Bn Royal Welch Fusiliers on front line and attack enemy on a frontage of 2000 x. Objective was line of trenches running N+S from L.12 central to L.24 central. D Coy on left, A Coy in centre and B Coy on right. Objective WEZ MACQUART. Attack timed to start at 1700 and a barrage put down on WEZ MACQUART from 1700 to 1715. The attack was to start by advancing in nature of peaceful penetration. B Coy was to clear up village and moving to South of it. Attack almost immediately held up by MG fire from towers in village and flanking fire from North down the old No Mans Land. B Coy reached the German front line but later was forced to withdraw. Enemy put down a heavy barrage on Bn HQ at DU BIEZ farm and on support Rd	Sheet 36 NW 1/20,000

17th Bn Royal Regiment

WAR DIARY or INTELLIGENCE SUMMARY.

October 1918

Army Form C. 2118.

Place	Date	Hour	Summary of Events and Information	Remarks and references to Appendices
WEZ MACQUART	6	0010	Situation as follows. D&A Coy in old British front line and Being in old enemy front line. The latter then relieved the 26 d Bn Royal Welsh Fusiliers in these positions. Enemy posts heavily engaged by our rifle and Lewis gun fire. Weather dull R.	
	7		Bn relieved of half its frontage by 26th Bn King's Liverpool regt. on Southern sector and engaged on D Coy frontage R. Weather dull.	BM 239
	8		Line advanced to old German front line RG. Posts were pushed forward from our front line to old enemy support line – positions established & consolidated. 2 LT Livingstone wounded RG.	
	9	1400	Bn still holding positions taken on previous day. Enemy raiding party 18 strong attacked one of our posts but was driven off suffering for 8 casualties. One of our men acting as carrier between posts was catured 2Lt Buckland	

17th Bn Royal Warwick Regt IV

WAR DIARY
INTELLIGENCE SUMMARY

Army Form C. 2118.

October 1918

Place	Date	Hour	Summary of Events and Information	Remarks and references to Appendices
	9		whilst endeavouring to release our man who was wounded in the leg. R.E.	
	10		Weather fine. Batn still in front line. Enemy much quieter. No signs of his having retired on this sector being apparent. 2/Lts Carlisle & Sargent rejoined batn. R.E.	
ERQUINGHEM SECTOR	11		Weather dull. Batn relieved in the front line by 26th Bn Royal Welsh Fusiliers & proceeded to ERQUINGHEM SECTOR in brigade reserve. R.E.	Ref Map No. 36.S.GRENIER 1:10,000 O.O 135
	12		Weather dull. Batn in reserve at ERQUINGHEM SECTOR. Casualties 2 O.R.s killed. 1 O.R. wounded. R.E.	
	13		Weather showery. Batn in reserve. Church parade cancelled owing to weather. R.E.	
	14		Weather showery. Batn still in brigade reserve at ERQUINGHEM R.E.	
	15		Weather showery. Batn moved up into right sub-sector and	O.O 136

17th Bn Royal Warwick Regt October 1918

Army Form C. 2118.

WAR DIARY
or
INTELLIGENCE SUMMARY.
(Erase heading not required.)

Place	Date	Hour	Summary of Events and Information	Remarks and references to Appendices
	15		relieved 25th Bn Kings Liverpool Regt. Relief good. No casualties. R.E.	
ST MACQUART	16		Weather wet. News received that the enemy had retired. Wiring order S.832/1 dated 12.10.18 was put into operation	S/832/1 dtd 12.10.18
			Patrols went forward at dawn and reported enemy had retired with exception of a few snipers	REF MAP
		1000	Attack Advance commenced at 1000. Objectives (a) & (b) of S.832/1 (Appendices) were quickly gained and at 12.30	See 36 NW 1 20,000 Ed 9a
		1230	Batn HQ moved forward to LA BEUVIÈRE FARM. This farm was entered cautiously owing to suspected BOOBY TRAPS. Orders were then issued for A & D (forming) Companies to advance on "C" objective. This was done and line J.19 central to J.13 central occupied. This line proved to be a strong position with very thick wire	
		1600	Heavy enemy shelling on field in front of Bn HQ (LE BLEU FARM). Casualties 1 OR wounded R.E.	
LOMMELET	17		Weather showery. Patrols pushed forward at dawn and formed "D" objective (see APPENDIX)	S/832/1 dtd 12.11.18

17th Bn. Royal Sussex Regt. October 1918

WAR DIARY or INTELLIGENCE SUMMARY

Army Form C. 2118.

Place	Date	Hour	Summary of Events and Information	Remarks and references to Appendices
LOMMELET	17	9.30	unoccupied by the enemy. Advance resumed at 9.30 owing to having received enemy verbal orders were issued through	REF MAP REFERENCES SHEET 36 NE
		10.00	by Brigade Commander that objectives were to be pushed on as far as possible. Tirlemont was to be pushed on as far as possible to canal bank 13.b.0.90 to 15.c.50.00 East of Chateau de Villers. An enemy aeroplane flying very low passed over. Fire was opened by B Coy and Lewis guns. In order to gain our objective artillery formation was to come into operation and companies were crossing previously abandoned and approaching LOMMELET the civilians rushed forward to meet us with hearty greetings. The commanding officer and 2nd in command were the first soldiers seen on the canal bank. Civilians were unable to cross to the west bank owing to all bridges having been destroyed. On this night the battalion was billeted for the first time for two months and the civilians	10,000

WAR DIARY or INTELLIGENCE SUMMARY.

17th Bn. Royal Irish Rgt.   October 1918

Army Form C. 2118.

(Erase heading not required.)

Place	Date	Hour	Summary of Events and Information	Remarks and references to Appendices
LOMMELET	17		Novelty was experienced of having an advance line with supports and reserves in billets. Total advance about 7500 yards. Casualties 1 OR killed RF	
LE MARCQ	18	0300	Weather fine. Orders received at 0300 to advance at 0900	MAP REF.
RIVER		0900	Advance resumed. A & C Coys and HQ having over bridge at N.21.a.2.9. K15 central and D & B Coys over bridge at	Sheet 36 N.E. E.O.S.A.
			Reception given to the troops while passing through villages in suburbs of LILLE was cheering and did much to encourage them. Badges Railway bridges were blown up by the enemy just before the leading companies reached them. Enemy MG posts were encountered and driven back. The Battalion then turned SE and excellent direction was maintained by A Coy on left under Capt Hytom and D Coy on right under 2nd Lt Weeks. Considerable opposition was met with on approaching the	B.M.349 B.M.252

VIII

17th Bn. Royal Sussex Regt. October 1918

Army Form C. 2118.

WAR DIARY
or
INTELLIGENCE SUMMARY.
(Erase heading not required.)

Place	Date	Hour	Summary of Events and Information	Remarks and references to Appendices
LE MARCQ RIVER	MARCQ 18		MARCQ RIVER with heavy enemy gas shelling of the village in C.28.d. and the environs of FORT DES MARCHENELLES. GOC gave verbal orders for support line to be established on line of LE MARCQ RIVER. D Coy, however, had already pushed forward and cleared FOREST DE LILLE & occupied the village. "A" company had pushed forward and occupied the line of the railway west of them, but as no touch could be secured on flanks orders were issued to withdraw to the river. Great energy and enterprise were shown by these two companies at the end of an exhausting days advance with intermittent fighting. R.E.	MAP R.F. SHEET 5 NE 1 20,000 E.D. 8a
FORZEAU	19	9.00	Victory fire Advance continued until at 0800 "B" & C companies passing through "A" & "D". "A" in support & "D" in reserve. No opposition was met with. Advance was covered our through SAILLY-LEZ-LANNOY and Bn H.Q. was established at FORZEAU. The outpost line ran just east of TRIEU-DU-PACT. Casualties 3 O.R. wounded (G.26.d.) R.F.	RECORD SHEET 37 E.D. 3 1 20,000 BM 363

17th Bn Royal Sussex Regt. October 1918

WAR DIARY
INTELLIGENCE SUMMARY.
(Erase heading not required.)

Army Form C. 2118.

Place	Date	Hour	Summary of Events and Information	Remarks and references to Appendices
CHAUNY	20		Weather fine. Battn moved on to TOURNAI-TOURCOING railway, reaching this objective at 1145.	
		1145	A barrage of our heavier Trench mortars of A Coy supported by a section of VICKERS machine guns went out to ascertain (enemy dispositions in woods on western bank of river L'ESCAUT (SCHELDT) & (ii) to effect a crossing at HAVRON. Enemy was driven from western side of river but it was found impossible to bridge the river under the materials at hand. Two rows confirmed [？] by O.R.E. D.V. Enemy post was engaged on eastern bank of river by M.G. & rifle fire and was put out of action. R.E.	BM 450
	21		Weather wet. Battn held up on eastern bank of river owing to lack of bridges. Enemy's reconnaissance from [？] back carried out. 2 Lt Wright killed (latest report received) R.E. 4 ORs wounded	" BA 600

17th Bn Royal Sussex Regt October 1916

WAR DIARY
INTELLIGENCE SUMMARY.

Army Form C. 2118.

Place	Date	Hour	Summary of Events and Information	Remarks and references to Appendices
TOUFFLERS	22		Weather showery. 176th Inf Bde was relieved by 177th Inf Bde. The Battn was relieved by Somerset L.I. and then proceeded to billets at TOUFFLERS (Q.23) R.E.	00/133
"	23		Weather showery. Battn cleaning up. R.E.	
"	24		Weather dull. Battn spent day in re-organisation & re-equipment R.E.	
"	25		Weather dull. Orders received from Bde. "Action on case of enemy invasion/arrival. Bn sends one hours notice therefrom." Route march in morning for remainder of Battn. Lt Col Barker CMG QSO relinquished command of Battn. R.E. Lt Col Ballard assumed command of Battn R.E.	S/859/1 / 25·10·18
			Weather wet. Church parade in morning. Concert in afternoon. R.E.	
	27			
	28		Weather sunny. Battn reorganises Coys into three platoon Coys sections. Platoon Guides parade of forms for COs inspection. Training carried on remainder of day with route march in morning. R.E.	

17th Bn. Royal Sussex Regiment October 1918

Army Form C. 2118.

WAR DIARY
or
INTELLIGENCE SUMMARY.
(Erase heading not required.)

Place	Date	Hour	Summary of Events and Information	Remarks and references to Appendices
TOUFFLERS	29		Weather fine. Training as usual R.E.	
	30		Weather fine. Training as usual. Divisional band played during afternoon R.E.	
	31		Weather showery.	
		2pm	17th to 1st Bn. inspected by Divisional Commander. Remainder of day spent in training. Officers 39. O.Rs. 766 R.E.	
			Strength	

N. Cullind Lt. Col.
Commanding
17th Bn. Royal Sussex Regt.

Army Form C. 2118.

WAR DIARY
of
INTELLIGENCE SUMMARY.
(Erase heading not required.)

17b/59 Vol. 7

Confidential.   Original.

War Diary
of
1ᵈ Bn. The Royal Sussex Regiment

From:- 1ˢᵗ Novr. 1918.
To:- 30ᵗʰ Novr. 1918.

F.4.

Army Form C. 2118.

17th Battn. Royal Sussex Regt.

WAR DIARY
or
INTELLIGENCE SUMMARY
(Erase heading not required.)

November.

Instructions regarding War Diaries and Intelligence Summaries are contained in F. S. Regs., Part II. and the Staff Manual respectively. Title pages will be prepared in manuscript.

Place	Date	Hour	Summary of Events and Information	Remarks and references to Appendices
TOUFFLERS	1.		Weather fine. Company & Specialist training. Lt Willard & 5 O.Rs go on course. Strength officers 39. Other Ranks 766. R.E.	
	2.		Drill & training occasionally. Training as usual. 2nd Lt Webb returned from course R.E.	
	3.		Weather dull. Church parades (Church of England, Roman Catholic & Nonconformist) in morning. R.E.	
	4.		Weather fine. Company & Specialist training until 1100. Battalion route march from 1100 - 1300. Battalion marched past Army Commander who congratulated battalion on its appearance and spirit.	
	5.		Capt Earl & 2 Lt Francies returned from leave & 2 Lts Labine from hospital R.E. Weather fine. Battalion ordered to stand to in view of a probable move. Order subsequently cancelled. R.E.	
	6.		Weather wet. Company & Specialist training. 2 Lts Carlile & Engg returned from duty with the artillery. R.E.	

Army Form C. 2118.

17th Battn. Royal Sussex Regt

WAR DIARY
or
INTELLIGENCE SUMMARY.

November

(Erase heading not required.)

Instructions regarding War Diaries and Intelligence
Summaries are contained in F. S. Regs., Part II
and the Staff Manual respectively. Title pages
will be prepared in manuscript.

Place	Date	Hour	Summary of Events and Information	Remarks and references to Appendices
TOUFFLERS	7.		Weather dull. Battn. takes part in a brigade tactical scheme - open Appendix I warfare attack. 17th Battn Royal Sussex Regts on the right, and 26th Bn. Royal Welsh Fusiliers on the left with an imaginary battalion in support. The enemy (1st Bn. Russian Guards) was represented by the 25th Bn "the Kings" (Liverpool Regt). (See 176th Infantry Brigade O.O. No OO1 d. 6-11-18). Brigade formed through outpost line at 1000 hours. The opportunity was taken to practise cooperation between infantry & artillery, machine guns & light tanks mortars. Battle ceased at 1230 hours all objectives being by then in our possession. 28 ORs taken off strength and 3 on strength. R.E.	Appendix I
	8.		Weather wet. Company and specialist training. 17th Brigade in line relieved by 178 Brigade who were relieved by 176th Brigade. This battn, therefore moved from peacetime support though the same billets were still retained. So by two companies and headquarters the remaining two companies moved into fresh billets at Chateau du Wawins. See 176th Bde O. No 139. dated 8th Rs.	Appendix II

Army Form C. 2118.

17th Bn. Royal Sussex Regt.

WAR DIARY
or
INTELLIGENCE SUMMARY.

November 1918

(Erase heading not required.)

Place	Date	Hour	Summary of Events and Information	Remarks and references to Appendices
TOUFFLERS	9		Weather fine	REF MAP Sh.37 Ed.3 Appendix III
		0100	S.862/1 dated 8/11 (orders for the advance) received from Brigade. Battalion ordered to concentrate and billets, ordered to stand by ready to move at half-an-hours notice. Orders to move (S.M.10)	
		1000	at 1015 received at 1100. Bn. moves route march to be Sclebe passing through BAILLEUL. Orders received on march to billet battalion for the night at QUATRE VENTS on east bank of SCHELDT there. Roads congested with traffic owing to the fact that two only are bridges over rivers for traffic on the divisional front. Two lorries transport was left behind and intention crossed the river by means of narrow footbridge necessitating carrying on single file width on account of five yards between each man. Rucksacks arrived on billets at 1930. Transport under 2nd Lts. Bramborough and Boatwright proceeded on leave	
QUATRE VENTS	10		Weather fine	
			Battalion in Fest line transport arrived at 0100. Battalion received	

Army Form C. 2118.

17th Bn. R. Fus. (Londs) Regt

WAR DIARY
or
INTELLIGENCE SUMMARY.   November 1918

(Erase heading not required.)

Instructions regarding War Diaries and Intelligence Summaries are contained in F. S. Regs., Part II. and the Staff Manual respectively. Title pages will be prepared in manuscript.

Place	Date	Hour	Summary of Events and Information	Remarks and references to Appendices
INRE VENT	10		Took up march at 0745. (See O.O.N.7 dated 9/11) advancing down to RESET on START 4. VELAINES near VERT MIRATS. VELAINES reported by 1100. Enemy not unduly possible that everything to run several of rations	REF. MAP. SHEET 37 Ed. 3 1/40,000
			arrived in VELAINES at about 1200	
			Orders (B.M.21 d. 10½) received from Brigade to reconnoitre in conjunction with 17th Bn. that carps had owing to congestion of open flanks retirements (s retired to a maximum extent was	
			CORNELLES at 1400	
			Scouts out of the line on the (B.M.25 d. 10½) cancelled. Patrols were pushed in VELAINES all roads very ill supported.	
VELAINES	11		Weather dull	
			Ration supplied up filling in small craters on roads. (B.M.32 d. 11½). Wire concentrating. Hostilities will cease at 1100 to-day Nov 11/18. Troops will stand fast in present positions. There will be no communication with enemy. News received quite calmly though later in the day numerous harmonium meeting the sittings band composed of instruments hidden, came in the ground during the enemy occupation paraded the streets.	

17th Bn. Royal Sussex Regt.

WAR DIARY
INTELLIGENCE SUMMARY. November 1918

Army Form C. 2118.

Place	Date	Hour	Summary of Events and Information	Remarks and references to Appendices
ELLAINES.	12		Weather fine. Batn. ordered to march to QUATRE VENTS as per B.M.43d. 11/11. March commenced at 0900 and arrives in billets at 1200.	
QUATRE VENTS	13		Weather fine. Bden engaged in cleaning up until 1100 & from 1100-1730 on a route march. Football matches organized in afternoon.	
	14.		Weather fine. Training in morning including range practice. Sports organized in afternoon and were very successful.	
	15		Weather Fine. Batn. route marched to WILLEMS started at 1035 and arriving in billets at 1500 (176th by Bde O. No 140)	
WILLEMS.	16		Weather fine. Batn. route marched to THUMESNIL on southern outskirts of LILLE started at 1037 and arriving in billets at 1500.	REF MAP SH. 37 / 40,000

Army Form C. 2118.

17th Bn Royal Sussex Regt   November 1918

WAR DIARY
or
INTELLIGENCE SUMMARY.
(Erase heading not required.)

Instructions regarding War Diaries and Intelligence
Summaries are contained in F. S. Regs., Part II.
and the Staff Manual respectively. Title pages
will be prepared in manuscript.

Place	Date	Hour	Summary of Events and Information	Remarks and references to Appendices
HUMESNIL	17		Weather fine & cold	REF MAP SHEET 57p 36 1/40,000
			Church services for various denominations RE	
	18		Weather fine	
			Batn engaged in reorganization & checking of stores RE	
	19		Weather fine	
			Company & specialist training RE	
	20		Weather dull	
			Company & specialist training RE	
	21		Weather dull	
			Company & specialist training RE	
	22		Weather fine	
			Company & specialist training. Education classification	
			Football league commenced RE	
	23		Weather fine	
			Brigade horse show. Batn takes first prize for best cooker & not first second prize. Football match in afternoon RE	

Army Form C. 2118.

17th Bn Royal Sussex Regt.

WAR DIARY
or
INTELLIGENCE SUMMARY.
November 1918

(Erase heading not required.)

Place	Date	Hour	Summary of Events and Information	Remarks and references to Appendices
THUMESNIL	24		Weather fine	REF. MAP
		09:30	Brigade parade in memory Distribution of medal ribbons by Divisional Commander to the following:-	SHEET 36 1/40,000
			Captain R.H. Lupton Military Cross	
			26082 Pte H. Harris Belgian Croix de Guerre	
			263126 Sgt. H. Darrell Military Medal	
			30133 Sgt. J. Cahill —	
			30560 A/Sgt. W. Mitchell —	
			30331 A/Sgt. W. Mitchell —	
			30940 L/C. W. Pinkerton —	
			30475 Pte. W. Goodyear —	
			A brigade church service was held after the presentation Pde.	
	25		Weather dull	
			Company specialist training. Education classes soon.	
			Football match in the afternoon Pl.	

WAR DIARY / INTELLIGENCE SUMMARY

17th Bn Royal Inner Regt
November 1918

Army Form C. 2118.

Place	Date	Hour	Summary of Events and Information	Remarks and references to Appendices
THUMESNIL	26 Thursday		Weather dull & foggy. Company & specialist training. Education classification. Cross country run in afternoon. Warning Order No 142 dt 26/11/18 received from Brigade re move to BARLIN area. RG	Ref M.P. 36 Sheet 27 40,000
	27		Weather dull. Training. Guard mounting competition. Lecture in afternoon officers & sergeants. Order for advanced parties proceeding to BARLIN received 658/C/1 of Brigade dated 27/11/18. RG	
	28		Weather wet. Thursday being a holiday no training was done. Transport Sports. RG	
	29		Weather wet. Training. Education scheme put into action. Brigade Football final. Have postponed to 2/3rd and later to 6/7. Visits to RFA & RAF. RG	

17th Bn Royal Sussex Regt

Army Form C. 2118.

WAR DIARY
or
INTELLIGENCE SUMMARY. November 1918
(Erase heading not required.)

Place	Date	Hour	Summary of Events and Information	Remarks and references to Appendices
THUMESNIL	30		Weather fine. Training for first hour. Remainder of morning being spent on education. Football in afternoon &c.	
			Education Scheme.	
			The scheme was worked out before the cessation of hostilities but was not put into operation until some time after the signing of armistice terms. Men were classified according to their general standard of education ① according to their trade ② for post education in the Unit. Men were allowed to choose themselves was compulsory ↑ subjects of education. All those who did not choose education were to be employed on the necessary fatigues and duties. So far the scheme has been very successful although there were large difficulties in the way of accomodation as materials to overcome. Instructors for subjects were discovered in the battalion both amongst officers & men, their leaving	

Army Form C. 2118.

17th Bn Royal Sussex Regt

WAR DIARY
or
INTELLIGENCE SUMMARY. November 1918

(Erase heading not required.)

Instructions regarding War Diaries and Intelligence Summaries are contained in F. S. Regs., Part II. and the Staff Manual respectively. Title pages will be prepared in manuscript.

Place	Date	Hour	Summary of Events and Information	Remarks and references to Appendices
Thetford			instruction in subjects for which instructors are not available will be given opportunities under arrangements made by higher formations. R3	
			Demobilization	
			Arrangements for the early demobilization of coal miners and railway workers were commenced during the month.	
	2-12-18		M.Callard Lt Col	
			Commdg 17th Bn Royal Sussex Regt	

Army Form C. 2118.

WAR DIARY
or
INTELLIGENCE SUMMARY.
(Erase heading not required.)

Confidential.

Original.

War Diary
of
11th Bn. The Royal Sussex Regiment.

From :- Decr. 1st 1918
To :- Decr. 31st 1918

WAR DIARY (17th Bn Royal Sussex Reg) Army Form C. 2118.
or
INTELLIGENCE SUMMARY. December 1918.
(Erase heading not required.)

Place	Date	Hour	Summary of Events and Information	Remarks and references to Appendices
LILLE	1918 Dec. 1		Weather fine. Church parade in morning for C of E. Non conformists and R.C's. Reinforcement of 1 Officer (2nd Lt J. Thomson) and 150 O.R's arrive. Battalion afternoon & Rail works. Results for 3 goals against nil.	1d.
do	2		Weather fine. Training one hour. Remainder of morning Education. Lecture by the Captain "Introduction to Physical Geography". Football in the afternoon A Coy v Transport. Result A Coy 3 goals nil.	1d.
do	3		Weather fair. Training one hour. Remainder of morning Education. Officers football 2nd vs. Glenwood left C.O. for S.O.S. Course at 17th Army School. Lt Spencer takes over duties as Battn. N.C.O.S.	1d.
do	4		Room one by 2nd Lt Jardine. Sgt Burton and Sgt Raven at Lille Depot proceed on return N.C.Os. Weather dull, sometimes raining one hour. Remainder of morning Education. Battalion held on 0900 hours to 1700 hours movements restricted for BARLIN area. Rations received for consumption on 5th & 6th inst. leaves open to 5/12/1918. Left for new camp 6 hours one order expected to new Camp. Lt Lechld cleared from hospital. Military Medal awarded to Pte POOL-, Sgt LOVERING, Pte O'CALLAGHAN, C/Sgt OLHAM, C/Sgt BREWSTER, L/Sgt TITCOMBE.	1d. App I
do	5		Weather fair. No training. Owing to Battalion under general fatigue prior to moving to new area. Transport left for new area. Football in afternoon A Coy v D Coy. Result A Coy 5 goals 1. Movements APP II Lieut. Bethetherness called 4/12/18. 2nd Lt Traine returned from leave.	1d.

WAR DIARY 17th B. Royal Sussex Regt

INTELLIGENCE SUMMARY. December 1918.

Place	Date	Hour	Summary of Events and Information	Remarks and references to Appendices
LILLE	Dec 6		Weather fine. Battalion embussed for MAISNIL-LES-RUITZ at 0930 and proceeded via LENS & BARLIN, detrained at BARLIN at 1430 and proceeded by march route to new camp. Officers accommodated in billets in the village and all O.R.'s in huts. All the Battalion in billets	
MAISNIL-LES-RUITZ	7		by 1600 hrs. Capt R.H. Lyle, M.C. proceeded on leave to U.K.	Wh.
do	8		Weather fine. Inspection of arms. Special leave allocation 1200 hours Battalion muster parade for bathing by Companies. Officer Remainder of day spent in cleaning and improving billets and camp. 2nd Lt. Lynch posted to A Coy for temporary duty. 2nd Lt. Reeman proceeded on leave to U.K.	Wh.
do	9		Weather fine. Church Parades in mornings for C of E and Nonconformists. Company fotball. OR grounds in afternoon. Lt. Bayliss reported from Base party in Bath Room.	Wh.
do	10		Weather fine. Training one hour. Remainder of morning Education, collect and efficiency tests received for draining party to leave to camp at RUITZ. Lce M. WRIGHT awarded M.M. Informant 10 Nov and at	Wh.
do	11		RUITZ. Weather fine. Training one hour. Remainder of morning Education. 2nd Lt Bowen & 80 O.R.s to new camp at RUITZ. Urgently wanted report for publication. Lt Lt Culverwell from leave	Wh.
do			return by 2nd Lt Culverwell on English War History 1685-1765.	
do			Weather wet. Training one hour. Remainder of morning Education. Lecture on "Business Methods"	

WAR DIARY 17th Bn. Royal Sussex Regt.
INTELLIGENCE SUMMARY. December 1918.

Army Form C. 2118.

Place	Date	Hour	Summary of Events and Information	Remarks and references to Appendices
MAISNIL-LES-RUITZ	Dec 11		Lieut Davies and Colours in Royal Tournament " by C.S.M. Hoyle. Gunners received their new theatre despatched to F.F.C. BOULOGNE. Performance of "Best Girl" H.Q. Cinema Hut.	
do	12		Weather dull. Holding love time spent improving camp. Officers football and theirs.	
do	13		Weather class. Reinforcements 25 Officers.	(A.T. Do Range) Th.
do	14		Weather dull. Battalion Boxing. Officers football 3 O/R's lost to 9 Gunners Coy in return match.	Th.
do	15		Weather wet. Training one hour. Remainder of morning Education. Afternoon football. Voice concert that event at R.U.T.Z. unavailable. Battalion to stay in present camp.	Th.
do	16		Weather dull. Church Parades morning football tournament afternoon Brigade Cup Local match R.S.R v R.A.M.C. Result R.S.R. w/o R.A.M.C. 3 goals.	Th.
do	17		Weather wet. Day spent on improvements to camp. Inoculations from Nucleus Course.	Th.
do	18		Weather wet. No Training. Inf employed improving camp and watching. 2nd Officer specials to A Coy to attend received on leave.	Th.
do	19		Weather fine. Further improvements to camp. Lecturers on Education. Questions on Election. Referendum Whole wings. Brigade bugle march R.S.R v R Welch Fusiliers. Result for not agreed. Gen. A. Rutherford from 39th Div. Who reported to D. Coy.	Th.

WAR DIARY 17th Bn Royal Sussex Regt
INTELLIGENCE SUMMARY. December 1918.

(Erase heading not required.)

Place	Date	Hour	Summary of Events and Information	Remarks and references to Appendices
MAISNIL-LES-RUITZ	Dec 20		Weather wet. Training one hour. Remainder of morning Education. Lecture by Lieut Davies "Finance of the War". Football in the afternoon.	
	21		Weather fine. Training one hour. Remainder of morning Education. Lecture by 2nd Lt Cartwright "English History 1715-1815". Cross Country run in afternoon.	2d.
do	22		Church Parade in morning for all Denominations. Afternoon football.	2d.
do	23		Weather wet. Training one hour. Remainder of morning Education. Lecture by Col. R.H. Lyster M.C. returned from leave.	2d.
	24		Weather fine. Training one hour. Remainder of morning Education. Afternoon football B coy v C coy. Result B coy - goals 6 C coy - goals. Building of central Cookhouse	2d.
	25		Christmas Day. Weather very fine. Church service for all Denominations in morning. Inner formation 13:00, all officers and N.C.O's serving. Engineers dispatch depart. Their men messes at 16:00. Afterwards Blandishments splendid. Greatest by Battalion in meet 2nd L Barrows in evening. Every body happy.	2d.
	26		Weather very wet. Holiday. Officers v Sardines somewhere in the evening. Centals mussing Started pulling am.	2d.
	27		Weather very wet. Baths for Battalion and delivery of clothes in morning. Battalion officers mis-dated 100 men availed the "CRUMPS" in pairs.	2d.

WAR DIARY 17th Bn Royal Sussex Regt
INTELLIGENCE SUMMARY — December 1918

Form C. 2118.

(Erase heading not required.)

Place	Date	Hour	Summary of Events and Information	Remarks and references to Appendices
RAISNIL-LES-RUITZ	Dec 28		Weather wet. Training as but. Remainder of morning Education. 50 more men received the CRUMPS at BARLIN by motor lorries.	24.
	29		Weather very wet. Church parades in morning for all denominations. During the afternoon for movement to HONDEGHEM followed by movement orders later in November, issued. Quiet taring in rations by central teaming. Order to give men extra pay. Also supper for 250 men.	24. App III
	30		Weather fine. During one hour. Remainder of morning Education. During the afternoon one half 2.7. Barrows Colorumeter 1 NCO and 1 man from Bn Headquarters dispatched with the Royal Welch Fusiliers. Due to lack of accommodation in reserve Coy was partly usefully each company with 1 NCO and 1 man from 76th Infantry Brigade received orders to move every to Royal Welch Fusiliers and return to camp. 17th Infantry Brigade were to Royal Welch Fusiliers and return to camp. Battalion Football Rest match from 0900 hours to 1000 hours. Remainder of morning Question Football followed by games. Lunch & Breakfast.	24.
	31		The Divisional Commander called at Bn Orderly room. During the month the light Pioneer wife attached carpentry classes did excellent work in the Camp. Making huts, making tables & forms, erecting Kitchens, putting stores into the hut, and many other additions for the comfort of Officers and men.	24

N. Pellatt(?), Lieut-Colonel
Commanding
17th Bn Royal Sussex Regt.

Appendix I

Administrative Instructions 4th Dec 1918

Ref the move to BARLIN area.

Transport complete moves by road tomorrow Dec. 5th.
Battn moves Decr 6th by lorries.

(1) All vehicles including cookers (less boilers as detailed below) will parade packed ready in 2.M. Yard at 1500 hours today

(2) OFFICERS VALISES:- Officers Valises will be at 2.M. Stores stacked by 1400 hours today

(3) BLANKETS:- Blankets will be retained by men at present

(4) MESS KIT:- Head Quarters and Coy Officers mess kit (less the barest minimum retained) will be placed on the Coy limbers and mess cart. Limbers & mess cart will report to H.Q. and Coys for loading at 1400 hours today

(5) BILLETTING:- Billeting last made to and for the night of Dec. 5th will be handed to the 2.M. today at 1600 hours

(6) RATIONS:- Rations for tomorrow the 5th inst will be issued today at usual time 1400 hours. Rations for Dec 6th will be issued today at 1800 hours and will be cooked tomorrow and issued to the men on the morning of Dec. 6th before starting. Rations for Dec 7th will be issued on arrival at new area.

(7) COOKING:- For cooking on 5th & 6th Dec Coys will retain 4 boilers each and H.Q. 6 Boilers. These only will be placed on the lorries on Dec. 6th.

(8) BAGGAGE:- It must be distinctly understood that the lorries on the 6th inst are only for personnel and not for baggage, or mess kits. Seperate arrangmts are being made for blankets

J. Cantland Captain. a/Adjt
17 R Sussex Regt

4-12-18

SECRET   17/Battalion Royal Sussex Regt
Appendix II   Order No C 19   Copy No 15.
                                          5-12-17
Ref 1/40 000   36 & 44 B.

(1) The Battⁿ will move by bus tomorrow Dect 6th to MESNIL les RUITZ in the BARLIN area

(2) Embussing place on road between Q 26.d.0.9 and Q18.C.4.0 facing South at 09300 hours

(3) In order of Embussing from the front, the Bⁿ follows the Kings Liverpool Regt.

(4) The Battⁿ will form up in mass in the R. M. Yard at 0850 hours facing the road, and will be divided on parade by the Adjutant into parties of 25 all ranks

(5) DRESS :- Full marching order S D caps worn one blanket will be carried by each man rolled, and placed on top of the pack

(6) CAMP :- Location of Battⁿ camp in new area J 36.C.2.2.
Sheet 44 B.

(7) BLANKETS :- Second blankets will be rolled in bundles of ten and be stacked outside the canteen (inside if wet) at 0700 One lorry will be available. Corpl Jones H. Qrs. will report at 0800 hours at Bde H.Qrs. and guide this lorry to canteen for loading. After loading he will return with the lorry to Bde H.Qrs and accompany it to the new area, and will be responsible for the blankets. Companies will each detail two men to be at the canteen for loading, afterwards to rejoin their Company

(8) DIXIES BOILERS etc Kept for cooking will be taken on the personnel busses

(9) BREAKFAST :- Breakfast will be at 0730

(10) 2/Lieut Goshawk will remain behind for at least 3 hours and be available should the Maire require to settle any claim He should report to the Adjutant today for details. also about train arrangements

(11) The Commanding Officer will ride in the first lorry also the Adjutant and cyclist. Major H Simkins M.C will ride on the last lorry

(12) Embussing Strength of all Companies and H Q Coy to Adjutant on parade.

(13) Acknowledge :- issued at 1200

Issued at 12·15 hours   J. Castled   Capt & Adjutant
DISTRIBUTION :-   17/Bⁿ Royal Sussex Regt
    Copy 1 Commanding Officer
     "   2 2ⁿᵈ in Command
     "   3 Adjutant   Copy 14 Signals
     "   4 OC A Coy   " 15 War Diary
     "   5 OC B Coy
     "   6 OC C Coy
     "   7 OC D Coy
     "   8 M.O.
     "   9 Chaplain
     " 10 2/Lt. B A Brigg
     " 11 2/Lt Goshawk
     " 12 R S M
     " 13 Corporal Jones

Mob. ref ee   14th Royal Sussex Regt   Secret
1/100,000   **Appendix III**   Move Orders by Lt. Col. L. Callard.   Copy No 17.
Lens 11, Hazebrouck 5A.   Nº C. 30.   December 29/1918

1. The Battalion will move to **HONDEGHEM** area by march route on December 31st and January 1st staging the night Dec 31st/Jany 1st at **ST VENANT**.

2. **Advance Party.** will be composed of 2nd Lt Braybrooks and one N.C.O. per Company with 1 N.C.O. & 1 man from Headquarters Coy. The party will parade at Battalion O.R. at 0800 hours December 30th. Their packs & blankets will be dumped at B.H.Q. & they will then proceed to starting point of 26th Bn Royal Welsh Fusiliers (Railway Crossing West of S in STA. North of BARLIN. by 0900 hours & will then march with R.W.F. to ST VENANT where they will await the arrival of the Battalion on Dec 31st. Two days rations will be carried by this party.

3. **MOVE.** The Battalion will parade on the road through the Camp at 0845 hours on Dec 31st formed up in column of route with the head of the column by the Quarter Guard in the following order. "C" Coy, "D" Coy, "A" Coy, "B" Coy, H.Q. Coy, 1st Line Transport, Baggage Wagon, which will be the order of march.

4. **DISTANCES.** 100 yards between Units, 100 yards between Companies, 100 yards between Unit & Transport.

5. **ROUTE** RUITZ — HAILLICOURT — BETHUNE — ROBECQ.

6. **HALTS.** 10 minutes to Clock hours.

7. **SUPPLIES** There will be a double refill tomorrow Decr 30th. There will also be a refill at ST VENANT at the ASYLUM on arrival. Supply wagon will march with the Unit.

8. **BAGGAGE WAGONS.** rejoin the Unit tomorrow at 1600 hours.

9. **BLANKETS & PACKS** will be stacked at Battn O.R. by 0730 on Decr 31st, 2 men per Coy will be detailed as blanket guard & will load the blankets on the lorries and will travel with them.

10. **DELOUSER.** The delouser will be taken to pieces and got ready at B.O.R. by 0730 hours on Decr 31st. Pte Shepherd will be in charge & will travel with the delouser.

11. **LORRIES.** Six lorries will report at B.H.Q. at 0800 hours on Decr 31st.

12. **BLANKETS, PACKS, & DELOUSER.** 2nd Lt Bennison & Sergt Bennett will superintend the loading and will be in charge of blanket party & will travel with the lorries.

13. **OFFICERS KITS** will be dumped at Coy M. Stores by 1500 hours on Decr 30th with the exception of the officers living in the Camp whose kits will be at Q.M. Stores by 0730 hours on Decr 31st.

14. **COMPANIES L.G. LIMBERS.** will be properly packed by 0700 hours on Decr 31st & will then be taken to Transport Lines by Transport Officer.

15. **MESS CART.** will report to Officers Mess at 0630 hours on Decr 31st.

16. **STORES.** Any stores which cannot be carried by the Unit will be brought to B.O.R. by 0800 hours on Decr 31st and a guard left in charge.

17. **HEADQUARTERS.** Three signallers and two runners mounted on bicycles will be detailed to move with the Commanding Officer at the head of the Column.

18. **REPORTS** Reports on the march to Head of Column.

19. **ATTACHED.** Advance Parties of K.L.R. 2/1 North Mid Field Ambulance, No 2 Coy Train will march with the Battalion at the rear of H.Q. Coy. and will join the Column at Cross Roads at J.18.d.4.3. (Ref 1/40,000 Sheet 44C) at 0925 on Decr 31st.

20. Acknowledge.

                                         J. Cartland.
0859.   Capt & Adjt
                                  14th Bn Royal Sussex Regt.

Distribution:—

Copy Nº 1 Commanding Officer	Copy Nº 13 Transport Officer
" " 2 2nd in Command	14 Medical Officer
" " 3 Adjutant	15 R.S.M.
4 O.C. Kings (Liverpool) Reg	16 Signal Sergeant
5 O.C. 2/1 N. Mid Field Ambulance	17 War Diary
6 O.C. Nº 2 Coy Train	18 File
7 2nd Lt S. Braybrooks	19 A.Q. 176 Inf Brigade
8 O.C. "A" Coy	20 Asst Adjutant.
9 O.C. "B" Coy	
10 O.C. "C" Coy	
11 O.C. "D" Coy	
12 Quartermaster	

Army Form C. 2118.

WAR DIARY
or
INTELLIGENCE SUMMARY.
(Erase heading not required.)

Original

Confidential

War Diary of

19th Bn. The Royal Sussex Regiment.

London | 1st - January 31st 1919.

17th Bn Royal Sussex Regt.

WAR DIARY
or
INTELLIGENCE SUMMARY.

(Erase heading not required.)

Army Form C. 2118.

January 1919.

Instructions regarding War Diaries and Intelligence Summaries are contained in F. S. Regs., Part II and the Staff Manual respectively. Title pages will be prepared in manuscript.

Place	Date	Hour	Summary of Events and Information	Remarks and references to Appendices
MAISNIL-LES-RUITZ	1.		Weather wet. Training in anticipation of moves from 0900-1000 hours. Education from 10.30-1230. Inter company football match in afternoon. 2Lt Bragg proceeded on leave. Strength of Officers 740 O.R.	
	2.		Weather fine. Thursday being a general holiday no training or education was carried out. Battalion running team completed a five mile course from mid afternoon. 10 O.R.s. Lt Talbot returned from leave.	
	3.		Weather wet. Usual training from 0900-1000 hours. Remainder of morning spent in education. Warning order to prepare for move received. Football in afternoon. R.E. Orders received for move to STAPLE. Advance party under 2Lt Graybrook detailed to proceed at 0830 hours on the 4th mounted on bicycles via HAILLICOURT-BETHUNE-ROBECQ. 2Lt Clarke + 20RO proceeded + 20RO returned from leave. Lt Locke joined Bn. R.S.	
	4.	0900.	Weather fine. Battalion proceeded from MAISNIL-LES-RUITZ by march route to ST. VENANT. The first stage of the move to STAPLE. The march was a successful one very few men falling out. These were collected and brought along by 2Lt Cartwright. Stores blankets were carried by transport. 15 additional lorries	
		1200.	Bn halted and were served with a hot meal.	
		1630.	Arrived at St Venant. Bn billeted in damaged buildings. R.S.	
	5		Weather very wet. Advance party as before proceeded via HAVERSKERQUE	

17th Bn Royal Sussex Regt

WAR DIARY
or
INTELLIGENCE SUMMARY.

Army Form C. 2118.

January 1919.

Place	Date	Hour	Summary of Events and Information	Remarks and references to Appendices
	5 (cont)	0900	Battn. proceeded by march route to STAPLE	
		1300	Bn. halted and were served with hot tea rations	
		1422	Bn. arrived at STAPLE and were billeted in and around the village. A proportion of the men were given 24 hours leave to for quarter-master billets in farm houses. R.E.	
STAPLE	6.		Weather fine. Bn. paraded by companies for cleaning of rifles, equipment in preparation for inspection by the Commanding Officer. 2 Lt. Talbot Greenwood returned from leave. R.E.	
	7.		Weather dull. Commanding Officer inspected of all companies + H.Q. R.E.	
	8.		Weather fine at times, relieved to stormy. Training by companies from 0900-1200. Educated from 1030-1230. R.E. Weather changeful.	
	9.		Sunday being a general holiday no work was done. Trouble in afternoon. 2 Lt Finney returned from leave. 2 Lt Iones & Lcpl Innes to Tank Corps. Lt Rodney joined Battn. R.E.	
	10.		Weather fine. Fatigue party of 20 men sent to MEERIS engaged in picking of manure. Party conveyed by lorries. 81 men departed to HONDEGHEM Repay Camp for duty and attached to 26 Bn W.Ch. Fusiliers. Lt Sg & 2 Lt Ebery return from leave. R.E.	

WAR DIARY

17th Bn Royal Sussex Regt.

PLACE	DATE	HOUR	SUMMARY OF EVENTS.	APPENDICES
STAPLE.	11		Weather fine. Fatigue Party for MESS non previous day. 6 O.R. proceed to dispersal camp for demobilisation. R.E.	
	12		Weather fine. Church Services were arranged. Church of England at 1000 hours. Nonconformists 1100 " Roman Catholics 0945 hours in village church. The hidden Means returned from leave R.E.	
	13		Weather dull. Training for first hours. 10-30 – 12.30 education Lecture by 2/Lt Curtis on the Monarchy at 1130 hours R.E.	
	14	0900 1030	Weather dull. Bayonet drill by companies. Lecture by 2/Lt Cartwright, Bn. education officer on "the history of the Monarchy". Locals in afternoon. 130 O.R. proceed to dispersal station for demobilisation R.E.	
	15		Weather dull. Practice in ceremonial for presentation of colours. 2/Lt Weeks & 5 O.R. proceed on leave R.E.	
	16	1100	Weather fair. Training as on previous day. 2/Lt Cross returned from leave R.E.	
	17	1130	Weather fine. Bn. paraded as per diagram attached for the presentation of the colours by The Divisional Commander. Major General Longatt VC. arrived for the ceremony. A short prayer of consecration was said by the Bn. Chaplain Capt. The Rev. Stafford, when the colours were presented to the colour party under Lieut. CRM. Fry by the Divisional Commander. A short address was then given by Major General Longatt VC.	

WAR DIARY.

17th Bn Royal Sussex Regt.

PLACE	DATE	HOUR	SUMMARY OF EVENTS	APPENDICES
STAPLE	17		reminding men of the meaning of regimental colours and that they stood for the then gave up a short account of the history of the Royal Sussex Regt. from before and during the war with reference to the hard fought by the 17th Bn. Royal Sussex Regt. The Divisional Commander then took up this tale and the writing there up the Bn. marched past which colours flying & pipes past the colours being retained on the Centre of "B" Coy. The Bn. was then halted. O. Coy. then marched the colours to the officers mess after which the parade was dismissed. Football in afternoon. R.E. Weather fine.	
	18		Training education as usual. Football afternoon. R.E. frequent. 22 Or. moved to HAZEBROUCK for demobilisation. Cpt Cardland + 2 O.R. Catholic forced on leave R.E.	
	19		Weather dull. Church parades Church of England at 10.00. Roman Catholic at 10.15 Noncomformists at 11.00	
	20	9.00 10.30	Silence in afternoon. 8 O.R. proceeded to dispersal station for demobilisation. R.E. Weather wet. Training by companies Education. Lecture by Lt Brown. Lecture by Major A. Simkin MC. + 2 Lt Brown. Lecture R.E. in afternoon. proceeded on leave R.E. Weather fine.	
	21	9.00 1.30	Bn. route march for other ranks. Education until 12.30. 12 O.R. proceeded to Richmond station for demobilisation. 2 Lt Tyrell proceeded on leave R.E.	

WAR DIARY

17th Bn Royal Sussex Regt.

PLACE	DATE	HOUR	SUMMARY OF EVENTS	APPENDICES
	22	0900	Commanding Officer inspected 8 Coy. Remainder of Bn. engaged in training P.G.	
		1030	Education lecture by 2Lt Cartwright on "Indication".	
			7PM proceeded to Dispersal station for demobilisation. P.G.	
			Weather fine	
	23		General follow up morning. Football in afternoon. P.G.	
			Weather fine	
	24	0900	Bn. route march.	
		1030	Education lecture by 2Lt Jenner on "British Empire in the 16th & 17th centuries"	
			Football training in afternoon	
			Thos Cahill Sergt admitted to hospital. P.G.	
			Weather fine	
	25	0900	Bn. route march.	
		1030	Education	
			Football in afternoon.	
			Capts Rylton & 2 ntho boys & Hampton's return to Bn for duty	
			Lt. Sallies Burrows & Ponfroke admitted to hospital	
			7PM proceeded to dispersal station for demobilisation. P.G.	
			Weather very rainy	
	26		Conducted church parade to Church of England and accompanied at 1000 hours. Roman Catholic parade service at 1015	
			Cold wet weather. Lt. Beverley, Lt Sinclair & 2ORs admitted to hospital.	
			10 ORs proceeded to dispersal station for demobilisation. P.G.	
			Weather dull. Snow melting	
	27	0900	Bn parade for physical training. Games	
			2Lt Cartwright & 30 ORs proceed to dispersal station for demobilisation	
			2Lt J Southern proceeded on leave. P.G.	

VI.
WAR DIARY.
17th Bn. Royal Sussex Regt.   January 1919.

Place	Date	Hour	Summary of Events	Remarks
STAPLE	28	0900	Weather dull. Education. Order received to prepare to move to DUNKIRK and then proceed to dispersal camp for demobilisation.	R.S.
	29		Weather dull. Batn. preparing for move to DUNKIRK. Part of batn. stores sent HONDEGHEM station.	R.S.
	30	0630	Weather dull. Batn. route marched to HONDEGHEM where it entrained for DUNKIRK and 0700 hours.	
		1630	Bn. arrived at No 1 Demobilisation Camp (IMBR DYCK Camp) previously run by 30th Bn. Northumberland Fusiliers. No1 Camp has a receiving capacity of 3000 men who are forwarded to QUAYSIDE for embarkation for England as soon as possible. 90 O.Rs. proceeded to dispersal station for demobilisation.	R.S.
DUNKIRK	31		Weather dull remaining. Batn. under instruction ? 36 th Bn. Northumberland Fusiliers previous to taking over the camp. Strength 37 officers 453 O.Rs.	R.S.

N. Allard / Lt. Col.
Commdg 17th Bn Royal Sussex Regt.

WAR DIARY

~~INTELLIGENCE~~ SUMMARY.

Army Form C. 2118.

Confidential

War Diary
February
1919

17th Batt. Royal Sussex Regt

Original

17th Battn. Royal Sussex Regt.

WAR DIARY
INTELLIGENCE SUMMARY.

February 1919

Army Form C. 2118.

Place	Date	Hour	Summary of Events and Information	Remarks and references to Appendices
MARDYCK CAMP DUNKIRK	1.		Weather cold raining. Battalion trains the adies of the Despatch Camp under the instruction of the 36th Bn. Northumberland Fusiliers who are running the camp at present. Brigade transport is pooled under Brigade control. R.E.	
	2.		Weather dull. The baton takes over No 1 camp from the Northumberland Fusiliers at 1100 hours. This camp receives men coming to Dunkirk for embarcation to demobilisation centres in the hutted lines. The men arrive irregularly and are arranged in drafts of 100 according to their dispersal stations. As soon as possible they are sent across to Tilbury or Dover. No stay in the camp of these men is seldom more than two days. R.E.	
	3.		Weather dull and foggy. L/Cpl Boutwley 1/2 R.S. Recover [unclear] return from hospital. It is with regret that the death from pneumonia of 2nd Lieutenant [unclear] is recorded. R.E.	
	4.		2/Lt Liedar & 3 ors. returned from hospital. Lieut Bottomly & 10 ors. proceeded to dispersal station for demobilisation R.E.	
	5.		Weather cold raining. 20 ors. proceed to dispersal station for demobilisation. R.E.	

17th Bn. Royal Sussex Regt.

WAR DIARY

INTELLIGENCE SUMMARY.

February 1919.

Army Form C. 2118.

Place	Date	Hour	Summary of Events and Information	Remarks and references to Appendices
ARDYCK CAMP DUNKIRK	6		Weather fine. Major A. Pinkerton M.C. returned from leave. 27 O.Rs proceeded to dispersal station for demobilization R.E.	
	7.		Weather fine. Capt Reynolds reported from hospital R.E.	
	8.		Weather fine. 2/Lt Sinclair proceeded to hospital. R.E.	
	9.		Weather fine. Church of England parade service at 1030 hours. Nonconformists Parade service at 1030 " 20 O.Rs proceeded to dispersal station R.E.	
	10.		Weather fine. The following reinforcements from the 8th Bn. Royal Sussex Regt arrived. Lt Col Paine 2/Lt O'Brien, 2/Lt Pemberton, A.E. Langridge, H. Lewis, L.C. Wilson. H.R. Williams and 142 O.Rs. the Battalion had by this time become very weak as such it was difficult to carry out everyday the work of the command. 2/Lt Earl balance went on leave. Capt Garland 2/Lt Knipe returned from leave. 2/Lt Sinclair returned from hospital. 10. O.Rs. proceeded to dispersal station. R.E.	

Army Form C. 2118.

17th Bn. Royal Sussex Regt. February 1919.

WAR DIARY
or
INTELLIGENCE SUMMARY.
(Erase heading not required.)

Instructions regarding War Diaries and Intelligence Summaries are contained in F. S. Regs., Part II. and the Staff Manual respectively. Title pages will be prepared in manuscript.

Place	Date	Hour	Summary of Events and Information	Remarks and references to Appendices
ARDYCK CAMP DUNKIRK.	11.		Weather fine. The Battn. reorganized on a 2 Company basis. A Company includes:- Bn.HQ, Pioneers, Tailors, Shoemakers, Police, Cooks, Officers Mess Staff, Officers Servants, Hospital Staff, Sgts Canteen, Interpreter, Dining Hall Staff, Vogel Station, Klinke ", Sanisart ", Commanded by Capt. S.R.Gilligwhite. 10 O.Rs. proceeded to dispersal station.	
	12.		Weather fine. 10 O.Rs proceeded to dispersal station 2 Lts. D.Carlisle & R.G. Lynell returned from leave R.E.	
	13.		Weather fine. 12 O.Rs. proceeded to dispersal station R.E.	
	14.		Weather fine. 10 O.Rs. proceeded to dispersal station R.E.	
	15.		Weather fine. 10 O.Rs. proceeded to dispersal station R.E.	

"B" Company includes:- Shoemakers Piece Cooks, Officers Mess Staff, Officers Servants, Hospital Staff, Sgts Canteen, Interpreter, P.M. Staff, Transport F.I.
Commanded by 2Lt. A.B. Brennan. R.E.

Army Form C. 2118.

IV
17th Bn. Royal Sussex Regt.

WAR DIARY
or
INTELLIGENCE SUMMARY.
(Erase heading not required.)

February 1919.

Instructions regarding War Diaries and Intelligence Summaries are contained in F. S. Regs., Part II. and the Staff Manual respectively. Title pages will be prepared in manuscript.

Place	Date	Hour	Summary of Events and Information	Remarks and references to Appendices
MOYEN CAMP DUNKIRK	16.		Weather wet. Church of England parade services at 1100 hours. Nonconformists parade services at 1000 hours. Roman Catholic parade service at 1000 hours. Capt. Griffin the Rev. returns from leave. 2nd Lieut. P & ors. proceed to dispersal station R.E.	
	17.		Weather dull. 2Lts Bennison & Thompson return from leave. 10 O.Rs. proceeded to dispersal station R.E.	
	18.		Weather dull & windy. 10 ORs. prs. ad dispersal R.E.	
	19.		Weather dull. 10 ORs. proceeded to dispersal station. R.E.	
	20.		Weather wet. 10 ORs. proceeded to dispersal station 2Lt. J.A. King struck off the strength having been seconded out to the U.K. R.E.	
	21.		Weather wet. 2Lt Ebdon proceeded on leave. 10 ORs. proceeded to dispersal station R.E.	

17th Bn. Royal Sussex Regt.

WAR DIARY
INTELLIGENCE SUMMARY. February 1919.

Army Form C. 2118.

Place	Date	Hour	Summary of Events and Information	Remarks and references to Appendices
ARDICK CAMP DUNKIRK	22		Weather wet. Reinforcements as follows arrived from the 16th Yeomanry Battn. Royal Sussex Regt. Lieut. W. Lockett, 260 O.R. Blagrove, H. Banham, all required 150 O.R.	
	23	7.00	Proceeded to Diekbuische station. R.E. Weather dull	
		10.00	Nonconformist rendevous service at "	
		10.00	Roman Catholic " "	
		11.00	Church of England "	
			260 Painter, +46 ORs proceeded on leave. R.E.	
	24		Weather cloudy.	
	25		260 Lt. Frame returned from leave. R.E. 220 Party proceeded on leave. R.E. Weather dull.	
	26		Weather wet. 260 Smith, Frame & 8 ORs proceeded to Hopkins Camp 260 Brian, Langridge, Cherry, & Hay proceeded on leave. Pte Wright A. awarded O.C.M. London Gazette Supplement dated 11/1/19. 13/1/19. R.E. R.S.M. Henderson awarded M.S.M.	
	27		Weather wet. Lt Col. N. Collard returned from leave. R.E.	
	28		Weather wet. 260 Strachan proceeded on leave. R.E.	

N. L. Collard Lt. Col.
Commdg. 17th Battn. Royal Sussex Regt.

WAR DIARY
or
INTELLIGENCE SUMMARY.
(Erase heading not required.)

Army Form C. 2118.

Original

Confidential

War Diary
of
17th Royal Sussex Regt.

From March 1st 1919
To March 31st 1919

Army Form C. 2118.

WAR DIARY
or
INTELLIGENCE SUMMARY.
(Erase heading not required.)

Instructions regarding War Diaries and Intelligence Summaries are contained in F.S. Regs., Part II. and the Staff Manual respectively. Title pages will be prepared in manuscript.

1919

Place	Date	Hour	Summary of Events and Information	Remarks and references to Appendices
Mantock Dunkerque	1/3		Batn. reinforced by 2 Officers + 205 ORs from Q.R.W.K. (7)L. Weather fair. Ordy Routine	
"	2/3		Weather - wet. Church Parade C.of E. 11.00 N.C. 11.00 R.C. 11.00	
"	3/3		Weather - wet. Ordy Routine	
"	4/3		Weather - wet. Ordy Routine	
"	5/3		Weather - wet. Ordy Routine	
"	6/3		2 Offs + 55 ORs reinforced from 1 R.Fus. Ordy Routine	
"	7/3		Weather - wet. Ordy Routine	
"	8/3		Weather - fine. Lt DMG Searle to A.O.C. & S.O.C. & struck off strength. Ordy. Routine	
"	9/3		Weather - fine. Church Parade C.of E, R.C. + R.C. at 11.00. Ordy Routine	
"	10/3		Weather - fine. Advance party proceed to Pont de Petit Synthe	
"	11/3		Weather - fine. Batn. moved to Pont de Petit Synthe	
Pont de Petit Synthe	12/3		Weather - fine. Ordy Routine. Lt Richmond appointed Batn. Shoots Off.	
"	13/3		Weather - wet. Ordy Routine. Interior Economy. 2/Lt baits Smith + Clavy returned from leave.	
"	14/3		Draft of 4 NCOs + 104 ORs arrived from 7 R.F. Weather - wet. Ordy Routine	
"	15/3		Weather - still. C.O's inspection of Batn. in full marching order. Ordy Routine	
"	16/3		11 ORs overseas to Depot and Station. 2/Lt May returned from leave. Weather - cold. Church Parade C.of E. N.C. + R.C. at 10.30.	
"	17/3		Weather - appr. fog. Ordy Routine. Major Scripture returned from leave.	

WAR DIARY or INTELLIGENCE SUMMARY

Army Form C. 2118.

Place	Date	Hour	Summary of Events and Information	Remarks and references to Appendices
at Petit Sythe	18/3		Weather - dull. 2/Lt Cahill struck off strength. Captain Webb & 2/Lt Langridge & others returned from leave.	
	19/3		Weather - wet. 2/Lt C. Smith reported from E.R.S.R. 2/Lt Blair proceeded to Depôt at Station. Duty Routine	
	20/3		Weather. Played in semifinal. Afternoon fire. Lt Cator & 2/Lt Jameson + 13 OR's proceed to Depôt at Station. Duty Routine	
	21/3		Weather - stormy. Duty Routine.	
	22/3		Weather - dull. Duty Routine. 2/Lts Milne & Wayne returned from leave. Duty Routine.	
	23/3		Weather - fine. Church Parade. 2/Lt Pinkerton returned from leave + 2/Lt Liles for approval.	
	24/3		Weather - fine. Batt. C.E. M.C. v R.E. at 10.30. 2/Lt Renown returned from leave move to Bavinchove Camp to take over from Res.B.	
Bavinchove	25/3		Weather fine. Oday Routine	
	26/3		Weather fine. Bday Routine	
	27/3		Weather fine. Duty Routine	
	28/3		Weather fine. Duty Routine	
	29/3		Heavy fall of snow during night & day. CO's inspection. 4.30 pm arrive Bavinchove Hospital	
	30/3		Fall of snow during afternoon. Church Parade. C.S.O 10.30. R.C. 4+5 NC 1173. 2/Lt Rennow, Johnson v Jameson proceed on leave. Capt Colquhoun returned.	
	31/3		Weather wet. 2/Lt Gove + 65 O.R's arrive from 1st R.F. to Division + 2/Lt Pinkerton approved. Maj. Shipton, Capts Carthew, Surgeon, Ellgood, Lts Lock, 2/Lt Atkinson, Evans, Denny, Knight proceed to join 1st R.S.R.	

N.L. Callard Lt Col
1st R.S.R.

Army Form C. 2118.

WAR DIARY
or
INTELLIGENCE SUMMARY.
(Erase heading not required.)

Vol 2

4 copies

F.12

Original

War Diary

of

17th Bn Royal Sussex Regt.

From :- 1st April 1919

To :- 30 April 1919

14th Royal Sussex Regt.   April 1919.

WAR DIARY
or
INTELLIGENCE SUMMARY.
(Erase heading not required.)

Army Form C. 2118.

Place	Date	Hour	Summary of Events and Information	Remarks and references to Appendices
Nadyek	1/4/19		Weather - fine. Ordinary Routine. G.O.C.'s inspection of Transport. Maj. Major Hardy D.S.O. joined for duty.	
	2/4/19		Weather good. Major Hardy D.S.O. took over command of unit from Lt. Col. Ballard.	
	3/4/19		Weather - fine. Ordinary routine.	
	4/4/19		Weather - fine. Lt. Col. Ballard demobilises. Ordinary Routine	
	5/4/19		Weather - fine. Lt. Gray, 2/Lt. T.C. Cooper, J. Birch, 2/Lt. M. Keen & 21 O.R. reported from 7th R.F.s.	
	6/4/19		Weather - fine. 36 O.Rs reinforcements from 7th R.F.s. Church Parade. 6.6.10.10 hr. N.C. 1110 hrs. 4 R.Cs 07.45 hrs. Baltic races.	
	7/4/19		Weather - fine. Storm in the evening. Ordinary Routine.	
	8/4/19		Weather - fine. C.O's inspection of new draft. 2/Lt Raines M.C. reported for duty. Ordinary Routine. 178 Brigade Mounted Sports at No. 5 Camp.	
	9/4/19		Weather - fine. 2/Lt M.N. Keen attached to Divisional School for N.C.Os. Lt. Col. G.T. Brooke, Welsh Regt, reported. Ordinary Routine.	Q.2.18.
	10/4/19		Weather - fine. Battalion bathes. Lt. Col. G.T. Brooke took command of Battalion.	
	11/4/19		Weather - fine. Ordinary Routine.	

Army Form C. 2118.

WAR DIARY
or
INTELLIGENCE SUMMARY.
(Erase heading not required.)

Instructions regarding War Diaries and Intelligence Summaries are contained in F.S. Regs., Part II. and the Staff Manual respectively. Title pages will be prepared in manuscript.

Place	Date	Hour	Summary of Events and Information	Remarks and references to Appendices
Handyck	12/4/19		Weather - wet. Major Hardy D.S.O. returned to Unit (25th Rigs). Ordinary Routine.	
	13/4/19		Weather - wet. Church Parade :- C.E at 11.00 hrs, R.C at 08.30 hrs. 14 reinforcements from R.F. 2/Lt J. Millbank demobilised. Lt F.C. Richmond returned from leave.	
	14/4/19		Weather - wet. Ordinary Routine. Capt A.V.D. Morley M.C. & Lt F.C. Richmond proceeded to join 6th R.W.K's. 2/Lt D.G. Lamb returned from leave.	
	15/4/19		Weather - wet. Ordinary Routine. Capt Bryatt M.C.M.M. reported for duty. 2/Lt C. Redman returned from leave.	
	16/4/19		Weather - stormy. Battn Route march. Lt. C.H.R. Smith demobilised. Lt. Q.D. Johnson & 2/Lt H.C. Thompson returned from leave.	
	17/4/19		Weather - fine. Battalion bathed. 2/Lt C. Redman demobilised	
	18/4/19		Weather - fine. Good Friday. Church Parade at 10.00 hrs. Football v. West Ridings in British & French Football Tournament (Result 3-3).	
	19/4/19		Weather - sunny. C.O's inspection of A & B Coys.	
	20/4/19		Weather - fine. Church Parade C.E at 10.00 hrs, R.C. 11.00 hrs. R.C 07.45 hrs. Replay of Football Match (2-2)	Q.T.R.

Army Form C. 2118.

WAR DIARY
or
INTELLIGENCE SUMMARY.
(Erase heading not required.)

Instructions regarding War Diaries and Intelligence Summaries are contained in F. S. Regs., Part II. and the Staff Manual respectively. Title pages will be prepared in manuscript.

Place	Date	Hour	Summary of Events and Information	Remarks and references to Appendices
Maretyk	21/4/19		Weather - fine. Easter Monday. Relay of Football Match (result 1-0).	
	22/4/19		Weather - fine. Battn Clothing Parade. 7 reinforcements from R.E.3.	
	23/4/19		Weather - fine. Rot Route March. Capt Lythone reported for duty as bath. adjt	
			2/Lt M. Norman struck off strength	
	24/4/19		Weather - wet. Ordinary Routine.	
	25/4/19		Weather - fine. Medical Inspection of A.D.M.S.	
	26/4/19		Weather - stormy. Battalion bathed. 2/Lt Greenwood returned from leave.	
	27/4/19		Weather - fine. Church Parade 6.C.M. 10:30 hrs, R.C. 11:10 hrs, R.C. 07:30 hrs.	
			Final of B.F. Football Tournament. v. R.S.O. Result 2-8.	
	28/4/19		Weather - wet. Men on Base employment recalled.	
	29/4/19		Weather - stormy. 190 ORs reinforcements from 13th Middlesex.	
	30/4/19		Weather - stormy. Ordinary Routine.	G.P.B.

R.P. Brooke Major
C.O. 17th Royal Sussex Regt.

WAR DIARY
or
INTELLIGENCE SUMMARY.

17th Royal Sussex Regt. April 1919.

Army Form C. 2118.

Place	Date	Hour	Summary of Events and Information	Remarks and references to Appendices
Nardyck	1/4/19		Weather - fine. Ordinary Routine. G.O.C's inspection of transport. Major C. Hardy D.S.O. joined for duty	
	2/4/19		Weather - good. Major C. Hardy D.S.O. took over command of Battalion from Lt-Col. Callard	
	3/4/19		Weather - fine. Ordinary routine	
	4/4/19		Weather - fine. Lt. Col. Ballard demobilised. Ordinary Routine.	
	5/4/19		Weather - fine. Lt. Gray, 2/Lts J.C. Cooper, J. Birch, & M. Keen 121 ORs from 7th R.Ss.	
	6/4/19		Weather - fine. 36 ORs reinforcements from 7th R.Fs. Church Parade 08.00hrs. W.C.1100 hrs. 2RCs 09.45hrs. Calais races.	
	7/4/19		Weather - fine. Storm in the evening. Ordinary Routine	
	8/4/19		Weather - fine. G.O's inspection of new draft. 2/Lt Raines M.C. reported for duty. Ordinary Routine. 118 Brigade Mounted Sports at No.5. Camp.	
	9/4/19		Weather - fine. 2/Lt M.W. Keen attchd to Divisional School for N.C.Os. Lt. Col S.F. Brooke D.S.O. Welsh Regiment reported. Ordinary Routine.	
	10/4/19		Weather - fine. Battalion bathed. Lt. Col. S.F. Brooke took command of Battalion	G.S.O.

Army Form C. 2118.

WAR DIARY
or
INTELLIGENCE SUMMARY.
(Erase heading not required.)

Instructions regarding War Diaries and Intelligence Summaries are contained in F.S. Regs., Part II. and the Staff Manual respectively. Title pages will be prepared in manuscript.

Place	Date	Hour	Summary of Events and Information	Remarks and references to Appendices
Mardyck	11/4/19		Weather - fine. Ordinary Routine.	
	12/4/19		Weather - wet. Major C. Hardy D.S.O. rejd to Unit (25th Kings) Ordinary Routine	
	13/4/19		Weather - wet. Church Parade:- C.E. at 11.00 hrs, R.C. 11.00 hrs. R.C. 08-30 hrs. 14 ORs from RFs. 2/Lt J. Millbank demobs. Lt S.F. Richmond returned from leave.	
	14/4/19		Weather - wet. Ordinary Routine. Capt A.v.D. Morley M.C. & Lt S.F. Richmond proceeded to join 6th R.W.Ks. 2/Lt D.G. Lamb returned from leave.	
	15/4/19		Weather - wet. Ordinary Routine. Capt Suyatt M.C. M.M. reported for duty. 2/Lt Redman returned from leave.	
	16/4/19		Weather - stormy. Batln Route March. Lt O.K. Smith demobilised. Lt A.D. Johnson + 2/Lt H.C. Thompson returned from leave.	
	17/4/19		Weather - fine. Battalion bathed. 2/Lt O.G. Renman demobilised.	
	18/4/19		Weather - fine. Good Friday. Church Parade 10.00 hrs. Football v. W.Ridings in British & French Tournament. Result 3-3.	
	19/4/19		Weather - sunny. C.O's inspection of A & B. Coys.	
	20/4/19		Weather - fine. Church Parade C.E. at 10.00 hrs, R.C. 11.00 hrs. R.C. 08-05 hrs. Replay of football match (2-2).	A.2.93.

Army Form C. 2118.

WAR DIARY
or
INTELLIGENCE SUMMARY.
(Erase heading not required.)

Instructions regarding War Diaries and Intelligence Summaries are contained in F. S. Regs., Part II. and the Staff Manual respectively. Title pages will be prepared in manuscript.

Place	Date	Hour	Summary of Events and Information	Remarks and references to Appendices
Maadyeh	21/4/19		Weather-fine. Easter Monday. Replay of Football Match (Result 1-0).	
	22/4/19		Weather-fine. Battn. Clothing Parade. Reinforcements from R.F.s.	
	23/4/19		Weather-fine. Battn. Route March. 2/Lt Rathbone reported for duty. 2/Lt Norman struck off strength	
	24/4/19		Weather-wet. Ordinary Routine	
	25/4/19		Weather-fine. Medical Inspection by A.D.M.S.	
	26/4/19		Weather-stormy. Batt: latted. 2/Lt Cranwood returned from leave.	
	27/4/19		Weather-fine. Church Parade. C.O. at 10.30 hrs, 2.C. 11.00 hrs R.C 9.30 hrs. Final of Football Tournament v. R.O.D. Result 2-0.	
	28/4/19		Weather-wet. Men on base employment recalled.	
	29/4/19		Weather-stormy. 190 O.R.s reinforcements from 13 Mdx.	
	30/4/19		Weather-stormy. Ordinary Routine.	

R.F. Bowden Lt.Col
Cd. 1/5. Royal Sussex Regt